Heirlooms of Ireland

An Easy Reference to Some Irish Surnames and Their Origins

Revised Edition

by

Joseph F. Osborne

CLEARFIELD

Copyright © 1998 by Joseph F. Osborne
All Rights Reserved.

First Edition, 1995

Revised Edition printed for
Clearfield Company, Inc. by
Genealogical Publishing Co., Inc.
Baltimore, Maryland
1998

Revised Edition reprinted for
Clearfield Company, Inc. by
Genealogical Publishing Co., Inc.
Baltimore, Maryland
2002

International Standard Book Number: 0-8063-4777-5

Made in the United States of America

To the memory of my grandmother, Ellen Conway O'Brien and my mother, Mary Ellen O'Brien Osborne, and to all the members of my extended family, both those who are and those who wish they were — Irish.

Table of Contents

What Are Irish Surnames vi

Acknowledgments vii

Introduction viii

The Counties of Ireland (Map) x

Provinces and Counties of Ireland xi

An Irish History (A Mere Grain of Sand) 1

Explanation of the Lists 6

Definitions 11

The Lists 12

Ireland in the 15th Century (Map) 153

The Irish Clans of Old 154

The Most Popular Surnames in Ireland 159

The Irish Chieftains: Now and Then 164

Notes 167

A Recommended Reading List 168

Surnames are heirlooms to be treasured and handed down from generation to generation with care and pride. Like an antique clock, a vintage automobile or an old photograph, the more one knows about the piece in question, the more one understands and appreciates its value.

ACKNOWLEDGMENTS

I wish to thank my wife Sylvia and my son Patrick for their moral support and assistance, and also Linda Addington and Peggy Larimer of Executive Office Service for typing, proof-reading and editing this manuscript and its endless lists of names.

INTRODUCTION

This book is about the surnames of Ireland and their origins. It is not intended to be an all inclusive atlas of information pertaining to these names, but merely an introduction to the tip of an iceberg. I do not believe, in all fairness, that the history of any family name can be adequately explained in just a few columns of background information. Especially an Irish surname. I'm aware of nothing Irish that can be explained away in just a few anything.

My reason for writing this book is that, hopefully, I will be able to entice some of my readers into adopting a more serious interest in their heritage. Perhaps by presenting this material in a somewhat light hearted format I will not frighten anyone away. No one will be required to memorize a lot of useless names, dates and places that they will never use (unless they want to), and best of all, there will be no quiz.

I am reminded of a young man I once met, who being aware of my Irish heritage, attempted to impress upon me the sterling qualities of his own Irish family. Had he not tried so hard to do so I may have believed all of the grandiose attributes he showered on his loved ones, but I had an intuitive suspicion that he was putting me on and I told him so. He admitted that he was not a fellow Irishman, and in fact, he wasn't really sure just what his ethnic background was. He said his family never discussed this sort of thing in their home, and besides, he didn't believe a person's ethnicity was important enough to be overly concerned about. He then proudly informed me that he was a one hundred percent American and that was good enough for him. I applauded him for his patriotism but I thought it was unfortunate for him that that was all he understood his ancestry to be. I found that particular experience to be rather sad, but it only supported my observations over the years that far too many people share that young man's attitude. I believe that everyone should be very proud of their heritage.

Yes, technically speaking, names are just mere words, a means of identifying a specific person, place or thing. But where do they come from? What are they made of? Geographic locations, occupations, hobbies, special interests, nicknames, and personal habits are just some of the seeds that are sown and eventually grow into permanent surnames. How we are perceived by others also has an influence on how they refer to us or describe us, thus sowing more seeds. How others spell and pronounce our name is also very important to its proper growth. As one can see a lot of work goes into making a name. When one thinks just how long it took for our names to filter down to us through many generations, I would say that that is a good enough reason to protect them as well or even more so than we would any of our other treasured heirlooms.

Tracing one's history back through time can be a very complex and time consuming experience. It is not impossible to reach a successful conclusion, but it does require extensive research, tenacity and loads of luck. There is however, the occasional path that leads to a dead end. In fact there may be a number of paths that lead nowhere and that's where stick-to-ativeness comes in. The more basic information one can gather before embarking on such a venture the better the chances are of arriving at a successful conclusion. Lost or destroyed records, name changes and name variations are just a few of the obstacles that are to be overcome by the family tree ferret. Fortunately for those bent on resurrecting their ancestors there are innumerable agencies and publications to assist them in their efforts to wed the present with the past. Before delving into the following lists of names, perhaps a brief account of Ireland's unique history will allow the reader a clearer insight into the obstacles he or she can expect to encounter.

Colorado Springs, Colorado
October 1994

THE COUNTIES OF IRELAND

PROVINCES AND COUNTIES OF IRELAND

Connacht

County Galway
County Leitrim
County Mayo
County Roscommon
County Sligo

Munster

County Clare
County Cork
County Limerick
County Kerry
County Tipperary
County Waterford

Leinster

County Carlow
County Dublin
County Kildare
County Kilkenny
County Laois (Leix)
County Longford
County Louth
County Meath
County Offaly
County Westmeath
County Wexford
County Wicklow

Ulster

County Antrim
County Armagh
County Caven
County Londonderry
(Derry)
County Donegal
County Down
County Fermanagh
County Monaghan
County Tyrone

Provinces - 4
Counties - 32

AN
IRISH HISTORY
(A Mere Grain of Sand)

There have been many major events that have occurred in Ireland's long and tumultuous history that have caused that country to evolve into what it is today. One would be hard put to attempt to single out which events have had the most profound and lasting effect on the people of Ireland. Four such events that have had a direct bearing on the surnames of Ireland are the coming of the Vikings in 795, the Norman invasion in 1161, the plantation of Ireland that began in the mid-16th century, and the arrival of Oliver Cromwell in Ireland in the year 1649.

The Vikings

It was during the year 795 that the ancient Scandinavians from Norway, Denmark and Sweden invaded the small green island located between the Atlantic Ocean and the Irish Sea that we now know as Ireland. These invaders, who were called Norsemen or Vikings, had full intentions of conquering the island and making it a part of their northern kingdom. Although they did not succeed in this endeavor they did raise havoc throughout the country for about two hundred years until 1014. [2] It was in that year that the Irish king, Brian Boruma, better known as Brian Boru, and his army defeated the Vikings during the battle of Clontarf. The popular Brian was killed in this battle and never realized his conquest. Brian is the acknowledged ancestor of the O'Briens. [3] Although the Norsemen did not achieve their goal of conquest and domination they are credited with establishing many of Ireland's seaports which include Dublin, Waterford and Wexford.

These Norsemen did not use family surnames which were passed down from father to son as was the custom in other parts of Europe. As a result of this there is very little evidence of Viking influence in modern day Irish family names. There are exceptions, though, that include the surnames O'Bierne, O'Doyle, MacIvor and MacKitterick. The prefixes of these names indicates that not only did they adopt the Irish lifestyle, some of them also formed clans in the Irish fashion. [4]

The Normans

In the 11th century England, Scotland and Wales were invaded by the Normans, also a Scandinavian people who had earlier conquered Normandy which is now a part of modern-day France. [5] After years of struggle with the Normans, England regained the balance of power over the invaders and the Norman barons and their armies became subjects of the English throne.

Around this same period in history Ireland was in the throes of a struggle for supremacy between the ruling kings in that country. Dermot MacMurrough, the reigning king of the Province of Leinster was overthrown by his adversaries and forced to leave Ireland. He fled to England and sought the help of King Henry II, who in turn authorized Dermot to use some of his subjects to regain his kingdom. Dermot recruited the assistance of a group of Cambro-Norman barons led by Richard fitz Gilbert de Clare who is better known in history as "Strongbow," to go to Ireland and take back Leinster for him. For his help Dermot gave Strongbow his daughter's hand in marriage and promised the Norman knight that upon his death (Dermot's) he would take his place as king of Leinster. Strongbow accepted the offer, realizing that in addition to his rewards from Dermot, the potential for a Norman kingdom in Ireland was a distinct possibility. Between 1169 and 1171 these Cambro-Norman knights not only re-conquered Leinster for Dermot MacMurrough but proceeded to invade the Province of Meath.

King Henry learned of Strongbow's advance on Meath and was well aware of what he and the other Norman barons were bent on doing. The threat of a Norman kingdom on his western seaboard as well as pleas from the Irish people brought the king, at the head of a vast army, to Ireland, and on October 17, 1171 he arrived in Waterford, thus disrupting the Norman plans. While in Dublin, on his return trip to England, the king received submission and promises of tribute from many of the Irish kings and bishops. [6]

Although the grandiose plans of Strongbow and the other Norman knights were dampened by the English king, the struggle for power between them, the Irish and the English continued for years to come. Many of the Normans gained substantial prestige and power over the Irish through their own efforts or as rewards from the King of England for their loyalty to the throne.

Eventually the Normans began to intermarry with the Irish and adopt the Irish way of life including their dress and language. Many of the Norman families even formed clans or septs in the Irish tradition. In time, these so-called "Norman Conquerors" gained the reputation as being more Irish than the Irish themselves. Norman names such as Barry, Browne, Burke, Fitzgerald, Lynch and Power are now among the most common in Ireland. [7]

The Norman period began as a disastrous time for the Irish, but like the Viking era, it too ended on a positive note. The negative side of the Norman invasion, however, was that it opened the flood gates for the invasion and subsequent conquest of Ireland by the English.

The English

England nominally controlled Ireland from the time of the Norman invasion. In practice however, for several centuries English law only applied in an area around Dublin known as the "Pale." This area consisted of the County of Dublin and portions of Counties Kildare, Louth, Meath and Wicklow. In the 16th century an Anglo-Irish parliament in Ireland acknowledged Henry VIII of England as king of Ireland and head of the Catholic Church in Ireland. This was the beginning of the "Tudor Reconquest of Ireland." To accomplish this the king began the process of destroying the Gaelic culture by outlawing the language, dress, and even the hairstyle of the Irish people. Because of England's determination to conquer Ireland, life in that country became extremely harsh. Being Irish in Ireland under English domination was most unfashionable at that time, to say the least. The struggle for freedom from English rule continued until 1603, when the Ulster clan chieftains gave into the English king and opened the way for the "plantation" of much of Ireland's territories.

The word plantation as we understand it in America had a somewhat different connotation at this particular time in Irish history. In the plantation of Ireland the native people were removed from their lands and replaced by colonists from England, Scotland and Wales. This scheme was highly successful in the Province of Ulster but it failed in the other provinces because there were not enough colonists to occupy the land nor enough labor to work them.

In 1641, there was another rebellion by the Catholic population of Ireland which included the Gaelic and Norman people. The rebels set up a rival government and ruled Ireland until 1649, at which time they were defeated by Oliver Cromwell. Massive confiscation of land and the forced transplantation of many Catholics to the Province of Connacht were carried out by Cromwell, and many of the defeated soldiers and others made homeless by the war were transported to the West Indies. The lands taken from the Irish were given to various "Adventurers" (those who financed Cromwell's army), to officers under his command and to others favored by the English establishment. The bulk of the population continued to live as they had before, but under new landlords who, for the most part, remained in England and controlled their nefariously gained estates through overseers. These overseers were, in many cases, Irishmen who, like their English counterparts, had little or no compassion for their Irish tenants. Consequently, life in Ireland continued to be very severe.[8]

In 1690, James II and William of Orange, contenders for the English throne, fought a war in Ireland with Catholic support going to James. James lost the war and large numbers of his supporters were forced to leave Ireland. One estimate reflects that over a half a million soldiers from James' army joined the armies of France and other European countries in the fifty years following the war. The soldiers and their descendants have come to be known as the Wild Geese. Although the Catholic army had negotiated honorable terms which guaranteed that there would be no general repression of Catholics, this treaty was not honored by the English. In its place a series of penal laws were enacted by the English parliament which severely restricted Catholic entry to certain trades, their right to bear arms, land ownership, inheritance and many other rights. In addition, the Catholic clergy was banished. By the beginning of the 18th century it is estimated that only about 5 percent of Ireland was owned by Catholics.

The penal laws are very significant from a family history viewpoint as they had the effect of reducing the number and various types of records relating to Catholic families by limiting the activities of the Roman Catholic Church, and by limiting the numbers and rights of its priests. The penal laws, in effect, hindered the keeping of comprehensive records. By reducing Catholic's rights to own land, they also removed Catholic families from being included in land records, such as deeds and leases. The penal laws also restricted Catholics from entering public office, removed their voting rights, and in general, impoverished them, thus cutting down the range of records which they might have been expected to have left behind. For this reason the 18th century is knows as the "Silent Century" in Irish family research.

The penal laws also applied in some respect to Presbyterians. This was a major cause of the migration of persons of this religious persuasion from Ireland to America and Canada during the 18th century. These Presbyterians were known as the "Scotch-Irish," the Scottish settlers who went to Ireland in the 1609 plantation of Ulster. [9]

By this time in history more English, French, Scottish and Welsh settlers had migrated to Ireland. In addition to these, German families from the Rhine Palatinate arrived in Ireland as well as families from the Netherlands and Sweden. A Jewish population had existed in Ireland for many years and during the decade 1881 and 1890, this population was greatly increased by the influx of Jewish families arriving from Poland and Russia, most of whom settled in Dublin. [10] At this point Ireland was well on its way to becoming a miniature melting pot in its own right.

EXPLANATION OF THE LISTS

The following lists are comprised of over two thousand surnames that represent just a handful of the people who reside in Ireland today and whose ancestors predate the Viking invasion of 795. The lists also include the descendants of many of the foreign families who migrated to Ireland between the 8th and 18th centuries. To provide the reader with a better understanding of the data contained in the lists, a more detailed explanation of each column is as follows:

Column 1

This column reflects the prefix to each respective surname shown in column 2. Prefixes with parenthesis denote those prefixes that are seldom used or are no longer used at all.

Because of the severe restriction placed upon the Irish during the 17th and 18th centuries by the English, many Irish families dropped the prefix to their surname. This was done to appease the English who had forbade the use of the Irish language which also included their Irish surnames. The Conways, Kellys, Looneys, Malones and Shannahans are examples of those families who dropped the prefix to their surname and never resumed them. There are many more families who did replace their prefixes after the restrictions were lifted.

There are some people who have the misconception that the prefix "Mac" is Irish and "Mc" is Scottish. This is false. The prefixes "Mac" and "Mc" are both used by the Irish and the Scottish. The letter "M" by itself is an acceptable prefix, however, it is rarely, if ever, used by either the Irish or the Scottish. The prefix "O," on the other hand, is used primarily by the Irish. There is however, a very small percentage of Scottish surnames that use the prefix "O". In addition to the aforementioned prefixes, the reader will also encounter the prefix "fitz." This is a Norman prefix that was introduced into Ireland at the time of the Norman invasion. The prefix "De" or "de" will also be found in the lists. These were used by the Normans, French and Spanish. [11]

Column 2

The surnames in column 2 need no explanation other than to alert the reader to the fact that the names are arranged in alphabetical order without regard to their prefixes. To adequately explain the many variations that are related to the surnames would require a manual of their own. Variations of surnames can evolve from a number of reasons such as spelling and pronunciation just to name a few. Often times a variation to a name may have no apparent relation to the original surname and to complicate matters, its cause is lost in obscurity. On the other hand, a pseudonym or synonym could evolve as a variation. The number of variations related to some surnames is quite interesting in itself. For instance, the Irish surname Gallagher (the g is silent) has twenty-three variations. There are at least nine variations of the Irish name Deloughery, and the list goes on. [12] Only a small number of these many variations will be included in the lists. The reader is encouraged to take advantage of the recommended reading list that can be found at the end of this book for a more thorough understanding of Irish surname variations.

Column 3

This column identifies the language from which the respective surname is derived. (See Definitions on Page 11).

Column 4

This column identifies the country from which a person bearing the respective surname migrated to Ireland. This column does not apply to the Irish-Gaelic surnames in the lists. (See Definitions on Page 11).

Column 5

The dates in this column reflect the century in which the first person or persons bearing the respective surname entered Ireland or the century in which the surname was established. This column does not apply to the Irish-Gaelic surnames reflected in column 2.

Column 6

The information reflected in this column shows the counties and provinces in which a surname originated or where the families of that name eventually settled subsequent to their arrival in Ireland. In some instances additional locations where a name has been recorded have also been included to provide persons researching names to have added options to investigate. (See map of the counties of Ireland and the list of counties and provinces).

Column 7

The data in this column reflects the definitions of the surname shown in Column 2.

Column 8

This column reflects the language from which the surname meaning is derived. It is interesting to note that many Irish surnames are made up of more than one word, some of which are totally unrelated. (See Definitions on Page 11).

Column 9

See column 1 explanation.

Column 10

We have already learned that many of the Irish were obliged to give up the prefix to their family surnames because of the stringent laws imposed on them by the English. A more complex and lasting issue arose when many of the Irish people were forced to abandon their family surnames and adopt foreign surnames or, preferably English or names that sounded English. In addition to the Irish adopting pseudonyms and synonyms many of the foreigners who had settled in Ireland also adopted new names. This may have been out of sympathy to the Irish, because they wanted to be accepted by the Irish, or any number of reasons. To further complicate matters the Irish also adopted other Irish names. Two of the reasons for this was when a clan or family name died out or was absorbed by a more dominant clan. Then, of course, there are always mavericks who have a propensity to be different. An example of this would be deLoughry in lieu of Deloughery. Of course deLoughery has a more Norman or continental flair.

In the eighteenth century when the restrictions laid down earlier by the English were lifted, many of the Irish dropped their pseudo names and restored the use of their original surnames, however some of them did not.

Consequently these false names became permanent family surnames and were passed from one generation to another, down to the present day.(13) The following are examples of some of these names:

Irish	English
O'Cleary	Clarke
MacGowan	Smith
O'Kerrigan	Comber
O'Murry	Morrow
MacRory	Rogers

If your name is the same as one of the above and you have always believed that your ancestors were English, you could be in for a surprise. You may be an O'Murry instead of the Morrow you always thought you were.

Column 11

See explanation for Column 3.

The original intent was to include the Gaelic spelling of all the Irish surnames shown in the lists but after considerable thought the idea was dropped. These strange looking Gaelic names would only drive the reader into hiding. The following is a list of five Irish surnames shown both in Gaelic and English that will help the reader understand why it was decided not to pursue the original intent:

Gaelic	English Translation	Gaelic Definition in English
O Heachthigheirn	Aherne	Steed, Lord
Mac Carthaigh	MacCarthy	Loving
O Dughghaill	O'Doyle	Black, Foreigner
O Cinneide	O' Kennedy	Head, Ugly
O Raithbheartaigh	O' Rafferty	Prosperity, Wielder

The above names may help bear out the fact that all of the Irish-Gaelic names reflected in the lists were originally written and spoken in the Gaelic language. It was not until the conquest of Ireland by England that the names were translated into English.

In addition to the many variations and distortions of Irish surnames that evolved in Ireland, there is one more obstacle that must be considered, and that is the arrival of the Irish immigrants in America. In the very early days, the Irish coming off the boats at the various ports of entry were not met with brass bands and throngs of people waiting with open arms to welcome them to America. In fact, the Irish were not really wanted in this country. As impoverished, uneducated and downtrodden as they were, they posed a serious threat to the American labor force. They did not come to America to sweep up the gold that lined the streets. They came, as many others before them, to escape the oppression and deprivation in their own country. In order just to provide food and shelter for themselves and their families they would do almost anything, including working for the lowest possible wage. This especially affected the Italian, German and other non-English speaking immigrants who came to this country before them. Another cross the Irish had to bear was their Catholic religion. This did nothing toward enhancing their standing in a predominately Protestant America.

The resentment toward the Irish became evident as soon as they set foot on American soil. This was apparent in the attitude of some of the immigration personnel who met the new immigrants as they came off the boats. Due to the lack of adequate formal education many of the Irish could not spell their names properly. The many accents of the Irish didn't help matters either. The immigration officials had little choice but to record the immigrant's names phonetically. If the official did not have a fertile imagination and the immigrant had a rather thick accent, the name could turn out to be just about anything. Poor Paddy O'Brien could become Paddy Oberon in a heart beat. [14]

Out of respect, fear, and ignorance of what the new arrivals believed to be the law, they never corrected their erroneous surnames. Consequently, many of these improper names are still in use today by their descendents.

Not many people care to trace their family lineage back to the Stone Age. Most of us are satisfied to go back only a few generations, just far enough back in time to prove to ourselves and to anyone who will listen, that we really do have some great, great, great relatives.

DEFINITIONS

The following definitions identify the abbreviations used in columns 3, 4, 8 and 11 of the lists:

1.	DA	-	Danish	10.	JE	-	Jewish
2.	DU	-	Dutch	11.	LA	-	Latin
3.	EE	-	Eastern Europe	12.	NF	-	Norman French
4.	EN	-	England, English	13.	NR	-	Norman
5.	FR	-	French	14.	NS	-	Norse
6.	GE	-	German	15.	SC	-	Scotland
7.	GR	-	Greek	16.	SG	-	Scottich Gaelic
8.	IG	-	Irish Gaelic	17.	SP	-	Spanish
9.	IT	-	Italian	18.	SW	-	Swedish
				19.	WE	-	Wales, Welsh

Prefix	Surname and Variation	Name Origin*	Migrated From*	Century Estab.	Geographical Locations	Definition of Surname	Language Origin*	Prefix	Pseudonyms and Synonyms	Name Origin*
Mac	Abbee	IG	-	-	All provinces	son of life	IG		Vesey	FR
	Abbott	EN	EN	14th	Dublin	pet name for Adam	EN		-	-
Mac	Aboy	IG	-	-	Donegal, Leitrim, Mayo, Sligo	yellow lad	IG		-	-
(Mac)	Abraham	IG	-	-	Cork	son of the judge	IG	(Mac)	Brohoon, Judge	IG
	Acheson	SG	SC	17th	Fermanagh, Wicklow	-	-		-	-
	Adair	SG	SC	17th	Ulster	-	-		-	-
	Adams	EN	EN	17th	Down	-	-		Eadie, Aidy	SG
Mac	Adams	SG	SC	-	Antrim, Down, Dublin	-	-		-	-
Mac	Adams	IG	-	-	Antrim, Armagh, Cork, Kerry, Tipperary	-	-		-	-
Mac	Adarra (- Darragh)	IG	-	-	Louth	blackman of the oakes	IG		Oak, Oakes	EN
Mac	Adegan	IG	-	-	Donegal	son of the dean	IG		Dean	EN
	Addington	EN	EN	-	Antrim, Down, Dublin	-	-		-	-
	Addis (Addy)	EN	EN	17th	Cork, Ulster, Westmeath	pet name for Adam	EN		-	EN
Mac	Adoo (-Cuniff)	IG	-	-	Connacht, Ulster	-	-		-	-
Mac	Adorey	IG	-	-	Antrim	son of the stranger	IG		-	-
	Adrain (Drain)	IG	-	-	Roscommon, Ulster	rough and firm	IG		-	-
Mac	Afee (Mahaffy)	SG	SC	-	Donegal	man of peace	SG		-	-

* see definitions

Prefix	Surname and Variation	Name Origin*	Migrated From*	Century Estab.	Geographical Locations	Definition of Surname	Language Origin*	Prefix	Pseudonyms and Synonyms	Name Origin*
	Agar	EN	EN	-	Kilkenny	-	-		-	-
Mac	Aghoon (Ahoon)	IG	-	-	Mayo	steed, black	IG	IG	Whitesteed	EN
	Aghy	IG	-	-	Tyrone	-	-		-	-
	Agnew	IG	-	-	Cork, Ulster	action	IG		-	-
	Agnew	NF	EN	-	Ulster	-	-		-	-
	Aherne	IG	-	-	Clare, Cork, Waterford	steed, Lord	IG		Hearn	EN
	Aidy (Addy)	SG	-	-	Ulster	-	-		-	-
	Aiken (Aitken, Eakin)	SG	SC	17th	Ulster	pet name for Adam	SG		Egan	IG
	Alcock	EN	SC	17th	Waterford	-	-		-	-
	Alcorn	EN	EN	17th	Donegal	old corn	EN		-	-
Mac	Alean	IG	EN	-	Connacht, Ulster	-	-		-	-
Mac	Aleary (-Alary, - Cleary)	IG	-	-	Antrim, Sligo	-	-		-	-
Mac	Alee (-Alea, - Clay)	IG	-	-	Antrim	-	-	Mac	Kinley	SG
Mac	Aleenan	IG	-	-	Antrim, Armagh, Down	-	-		Lyness	EN
Mac	Aleer	IG	-	-	Tyrone	dun-colored, weather beaten	IG		-	-
Mac	Aleese (-Ileese, -Leese, -Lice)	IG	-	-	Cork, Derry	son of the devotee of Jesus	IG		Gillis	SG
Mac	Aleevy	IG	-	-	Donegal, Down	-	-	(Mac)	Dunlevy	IG

* see definitions

Prefix	Surname and Variation	Name Origin*	Migrated From*	Century Estab.	Geographical Locations	Definition of Surname	Language Origin*	Prefix	Pseudonyms and Synonyms	Name Origin*
	Aleman	NF	EN	-	Kerry	-	-		-	-
	Alexander	EN	EN	-	Antrim, Down	-	-		-	-
Mac	Ally	IG	-	-	Fermanagh	-	-		Lilly	EN
Mac	Alindon	IG	-	-	Armagh, Down	devotee of St. Finian	IG		Leonard	EN
Mac	Alinion (Aleenen)	IG	-	-	Fermanagh	devotee of St. Finian	IG		Leonard	EN
Mac	Alister (-Allister)	IG	SC	14th	Ulster	-	-		-	-
Mac	Alivery	IG	-	-	Tyrone	winter	IG	Mac	Aleenen Winter	IG EN
Mac	Allen	SG	SC	16th	Derry, Donegal	rock	SG		-	-
	Allen	EN	EN	-	Tipperary	-	-	(O)	Hallion	IG
	Alley	NS	EN	16th	Kildare, Laois	-	-		-	-
	Allman	GE	NR	12th	Kerry, Louth	-	-		Almond	EN
Mac	Aloon	IG	-	-	Donegal, Fermanagh Tyrone	Monday	IG		Monday	EN
Mac	Alpin (-Calpin)	SG	SC	-	Ulster	lump	SG		-	-
	Altimas	GE	-	18th	Wexford	-	-		Alton	NF
	Alymer	GE	EN	13th	Dublin, Kildare, Meath	-	-		-	-
	Ambrose	IG	-	-	Cork, Limerick, Wexford	-	-		-	-
Mac	Amore	IG	-	-	Wexford	-	-		Davis	WE
	Anboro	NF	EN	-	Louth	-	-		-	-

* see definitions

Prefix	Surname and Variation	Name Origin*	Migrated From*	Century Estab.	Geographical Locations	Definition of Surname	Language Origin*	Prefix	Pseudonyms and Synonyms	Name Origin*
	Anderson	EN	EN	-	Ulster	son of Andrew	EN		-	-
	Andrews	EN	EN	17th	All Providences	-	-		-	-
Mac	Andrews	IG	-	-	Mayo	son of Andrew	IG		Andrews	EN
Mac	Aneany (-Eneany, Neeny)	IG	-	-	Monaghan, Roscommon	dean	IG		Bird Rabbit	EN EN
Mac	Anespie (Aspig)	IG	-	-	Tyrone	son of the bishop	IG		Bishop	EN
Mac	Ann	IG	-	-	Clare, Limerick	-	-		-	-
	Annesley	EN	EN	17th	All Provinces	diminutive of Ann	EN		-	-
	Annett	EN	EN	17th	Down	-	-		-	-
	Anthony	EN	EN	17th	Waterford	-	-		-	-
	Archbold (Archibald)	EN	EN	-	Wicklow	-	-		Aspel	EN
	Archdale	EN	EN	17th	Fermanagh	-	-		-	-
	Archdeacon	NF	EN	13th	Kilkenny	-	-		Cody	IG
	Archer	NF	EN	13th	Kilkenny	-	-		Orchard	EN
de	Arcy (Darcy)	IG	-	-	Meath	-	-		-	-
	Ardagh	IG	-	-	Louth, Waterford	-	-		-	-
Mac	Ardle	IG	-	-	Monaghan	high valor	IG		Grey	EN
Mac	Areavy (- Gilreevy, - Ilreavy)	IG	-	-	Antrim, Down	grey or brindled	IG		-	-
Mac	Aree	IG	-	-	Monaghan	manly, king	IG		King	EN
Mac	Argue	IG	-	-	Cavan	-	-		-	-

* see definitions

Prefix	Surname and Variation	Name Origin*	Migrated From*	Century Estab.	Geographical Locations	Definition of Surname	Language Origin*	Prefix	Pseudonyms and Synonyms	Name Origin*
(O)	Arkins	IG	-	-	Clare	-	-		-	-
	Armitage	EN	EN	17th	Cork, Louth, Offaly, Tipperary	hermitage	EN		-	-
	Armstrong	EN	EN	-	Ulster	-	-		-	-
	Arnold	EN	EN	13th	Dublin, Ulster	-	-		-	-
	Arnott	SG	SC	-	Antrim	-	-		-	-
Mac	Artan (- Cartan)	IG	-	-	Down	derived from personal name Art	IG		-	-
	Arthur	NS	-	12th	Limerick	-	-		Arthur	NF
Mac	Arthur (-Carter)	SG	SC	-	Limerick	son of Arthur	SG		-	-
	Arundel (Aringale)	EN	EN	13th	Cork	-	-		-	-
Mac	Ashe	EN	EN	14th	Kildare, Meath	dweller by the ash trees	EN		-	-
	Ashinagh	IG	-	-	Armagh, Donegal, Meath	fox	IG		Fox	EN
Mac	Atee	IG	-	-	Armagh, Monaghan	-	-		-	-
Mac	Ateer	IG	-	-	Armagh, Fermanagh	craftsman	IG	Mac	Intyre Wright Freeman Carpenter	SG EN EN EN
	Athy	NF	EN	14th	Kildare, Meath	-	-		-	-
Mac	Atilla (Tully)	IG	-	-	Cavan, Longford	flood	IG		Flood	EN
	Atkins	EN	EN	17th	Cork	pet name for Adam	EN		-	-

Prefix	Surname and Variation	Name Origin*	Migrated From*	Century Estab.	Geographical Locations	Definition of Surname	Language Origin*	Prefix	Pseudonyms and Synonyms	Name Origin*
	Atkinson	EN	EN	-	Ulster	pet name for Adam	EN		-	-
Mac	Auley (Awley, Cawley)	IG	-	-	Fermanagh, Offaly, Westmeath	-	-		-	-
Mac	Auliffe	IG	-	-	Cork	-	-		-	-
	Aungier	FR	-	17th	Dublin, Longford, Offaly	-	-		Danger	EN
	Austin	EN	EN	14th	Connacht, Ulster	-	-		-	-
Mac	Avaddy	IG	-	-	Mayo	dog	IG	(O)	Madden	IG
Mac	Avenue	IG	-	-	Derry	-	-		-	-
Mac	Avinchey	IG	-	-	Armagh, Derry, Tyrone	-	-		Vincent	EN
Mac	Avoy	IG	-	-	Connacht, Ulster	woodman	IG		-	-
	Aylward	NF	EN	14th	Kilkenny, Waterford	-	-		Elward	EN
	Ayres (Eyres)	EN	EN	-	Galway, Waterford	-	-		-	-
de	Baa	NF	EN	12th	Dublin, Louth, Meath	-	-		Bath	NF
	Babe (La Babbe)	NF	EN	-	Louth	guileless disposition	NF		-	-
	Bacon (La Bacoun)	NF	EN	-	Meath	the pig (pig keeper)	NF		-	-
	Badger	EN	EN	-	Galway, Kerry	-	-		-	-
	Badigan	IG	-	-	Donegal, Monaghan	-	-		-	-
(O)	Bagnall	EN	EN	-	Carlow	-	-		-	-
	Bagot	GE	-	16th	Dublin, Limerick	-	-		-	-
	Bailey (Baille)	EN	EN	13th	Leinster, Munster, Ulster	-	-		-	-

* see definitions

Prefix	Surname and Variation	Name Origin*	Migrated From*	Century Estab.	Geographical Locations	Definition of Surname	Language Origin*	Prefix	Pseudonyms and Synonyms	Name Origin*
	Baird	SG	SC	-	Antrim, Down	poet	SG		-	-
	Baker	EN	EN	13th	All Provinces	baker	EN		-	-
	Baldrick (Boldrick)	EN	EN	17th	Donegal	bold rule	EN		-	-
	Baldwin (Baldoon, Boden, Bodkin)	GE	GE	15th	Donegal, Waterford	bold friend	GE		-	-
	Ball	EN	EN	-	Leinster, Ulster	-	-		-	-
	Ballagh	IG	-	-	All Provinces	speckled, marked	IG		-	-
	Ballentine	SG	SC	-	Ulster	-	-		-	-
	Ballinger	FR	EN	-	Clare	-	-		-	-
(O)	Banane	IG	-	-	Fermanagh, Offaly	-	-		-	-
(O)	Bane (Bawn)	IG	-	-	Clare, Galway	white, woman	IG		Bayne White	EN EN
	Banigan	IG	-	-	Donegal, Monaghan	-	-		-	-
(O)	Banks	EN	EN	-	Offaly	-	-		-	-
	Bannister	FR	-	17th	Carlow, Cork	basket	FR		-	-
(O)	Bannon (Banane)	IG	-	-	Fermanagh, Mayo, Offaly	-	-		Bunyon White	EN EN
	Barber (Barbour)	NF	EN	13th	Cork, Down, Dublin	-	-		-	-
	Barclay (Barkley)	EN	EN	16th	Ulster	-	-		-	-
(O)	Bardon (Barden, Bardane)	IG	-	-	Longford, Waterford Westmeath, Wexford	bard (poet)	IG		Barnes	EN

* see definitions

Prefix	Surname and Variation	Name Origin*	Migrated From*	Century Estab.	Geographical Locations	Definition of Surname	Language Origin*	Prefix	Pseudonyms and Synonyms	Name Origin*
	Barker	EN	EN	16th	Dublin, Leinster, Ulster	tree stripper	EN		-	-
	Barnacle	EN	EN	-	Mayo	-	-		-	-
(O)	Barnane	IG	-	-	Cork	-	-		Bernard / Barron	GE / IG
	Barnes	EN	EN	-	All Provinces	-	-		-	-
	Barneville (Barnewall)	NF	EN	-	Dublin, Meath	-	-		Bernal / Burnell	NF / NF
	Barr	EN / SG	EN / SC	-	Cork, Ulster	-	-		-	-
	Barr	NF	EN	-	Cork, Limerick	-	-		-	-
	Barrett	NF	EN	13th	Cork, Mayo	-	-	Mac	Padden	IG
	Barrington	EN	EN	-	Cork, Laois	-	-		-	-
	Barron	IG	-	-	Kilkenny, Waterford	-	-		Barnes / Barrington	EN / EN
Mac	Barron	SG	SC	-	Armagh	-	-		-	-
	Barton	EN	EN	13th	Kildare	-	-		-	-
(O)	Baskin	IG	-	-	Clare, Cork	-	-		-	-
	Bassett	FR	-	13th	Not closely associated with any particular area	of low stature	FR		-	-
	Bateman	EN	EN	13th	Cork	servant of Bartholomew	EN		-	-
	Bates	EN	EN	17th	Dublin, Ulster	-	-		-	-
	Bathe	NF	EN	-	Leinster	-	-		-	-
	Baxter	SG	SC	-	Ulster	baker	SG		-	-
Mac	Bay (Bey)	SG	SC	-	Ulster	-	-		-	-

* see definitions

Prefix	Surname and Variation	Name Origin*	Migrated From*	Century Estab.	Geographical Locations	Definition of Surname	Language Origin*	Prefix	Pseudonyms and Synonyms	Name Origin*
Mac	Bean	IG	-	-	Laois, Offaly	-	-		-	-
(O)	Beary	IG	-	-	Offaly	-	-		Berry	EN
	Beatty (Beatagh, Betagh, Betty)	SG	SC	-	Meath, Ulster	public victualler (provider of food)	SG		-	-
	Beaumont	GE	-	-	Limerick, Ulster	-	-		Bowman	GE
	Beckett	FR	EN	15th	Leinster, Ulster	-	-		-	-
	Begg(e) (Beggs, Bigge)	NF	EN	-	Cork, Leinster	small	NF		Small	EN
(O)	Begley	IG	-	-	Cork, Donegal, Kerry	little, hero	IG		Bagley	EN
(O)	Beglin	IG	-	-	Longford, Westmeath	little, scholarship	IG		Bagnall	EN
(O)	Behan (Beaghan)	IG	-	-	Clare, Kerry, Kildare	bee	IG		-	-
(O)	Beirne	NS	-	-	Mayo, Roscommon	derived from the Norse forename Bjorn	NS		Burns Byron	SG EN
	Bell	FR	EN	12th	Ulster	beautiful	FR		-	-
	Bellew	NF	EN	13th	Galway, Louth, Meath	-	-		Bailey Baillie	EN EN
	Belton	EN	EN	17th	Leinster	-	-		Weldon	NF
	Bennett	FR	EN	14th	Kilkenny	blessed	LA		Bunyan	EN
	Benson (Benison)	EN	EN	-	Antrim, Down, Dublin	-	-		-	-
	Bentley	EN	EN	17th	Clare, Limerick	-	-		-	-
(O)	Bergin (Bergan, Berrigan)	IG	-	-	Laois, Offaly	wondrous birth	IG		-	-

* see definitions

Prefix	Surname and Variation	Name Origin*	Migrated From*	Century Estab.	Geographical Locations	Definition of Surname	Language Origin*	Prefix	Pseudonyms and Synonyms	Name Origin*
	Berle	NS	-	-	Louth	reddish brown complexion	NS		-	-
	Bermingham	NF	EN	-	Galway, Kildare		-		Corish	IG
(O)	Bernard	EN	EN	-	Cork		-			-
	Berrane (Birrane)	IG	-	-	Mayo	spear	IG		Byrne / Byron / Barron	IG / EN / IG
	Berry (Bury, Beary)	EN	EN	17th	All Provinces		-			-
	Best	EN	EN	17th	Antrim, Armagh, Carlow, Tyrone		EN			-
Mac	Beth	SG	SC	-	Ulster	beast, one in charge of cattle	SG			-
	Bethel	WE	-	17th	Ulster	life				-
(O)	Biggane (Biggins)	IG	-	-	Mayo, Monaghan	little	IG		Little / Littleton	EN / EN
(O)	Biggy	IG	-	-	Mayo	small	IG		Small	EN
	Binane	IG	-	-	Kerry		-		Bunyan	EN
	Bingham	EN	EN	-	Mayo, Ulster		-			-
	Bird	EN	EN	-	Armagh		-			-
Mac	Birney	NS	SC	-	Ulster		-			-
	Biscaro	IT	-	-	Antrim, Down, Dublin		-			-
	Bishop	EN	EN	-	Donegal, Down, Galway, Louth		-			-
	Bissett	SG	SC	-	Antrim		-	Mac	Keown	IG
	Black	SG	SC	-	Ulster		-			-

* see definitions

Prefix	Surname and Variation	Name Origin*	Migrated From*	Century Estab.	Geographical Locations	Definition of Surname	Language Origin*	Prefix	Pseudonyms and Synonyms	Name Origin*
	Blackall (Blackhall)	EN	EN	17th	Clare, Dublin, Limerick, Ulster	dweller by the black nook	EN		-	-
	Blackburn(e) (Blackbyrne)	EN	EN	14th	Donegal, Meath, Roscommon	-	-		-	-
	Blair	SG	SC	-	Ulster	-	-		-	-
	Blake	EN	EN	13th	Galway, Kildare	black	EN		Caddell	WE
	Blaney (Blayney)	WE	WE	16th	Monaghan	-	-		-	-
(O)	Bleahan (Bleheen)	IG	-	-	Galway	-	-		Melvin	IG
	Blennerhassett	EN	EN	16th	Fermanagh, Kerry	-	-		Hassett	IG
	Blessing	EN	EN	-	Leitrim	-	-		-	-
	Bligh	NS	NS	-	Connacht	blithe	-		-	-
	Blood	WE	EN	16th	Clare	-	-		-	-
	Bloomer	EN	EN	-	Donegal, Mayo, Roscommon, Tyrone	-	-		-	-
	Blowick	IG	-	-	Fermanagh, Mayo	fame - son	IG		Blake	EN
	Blunt	NF	EN	-	Kerry, Louth	blond or fair haired	NF		White	EN
	Boal (Boles, Bowles)	EN	EN	-	Antrim, Down	-	-		-	-
	Bodkin	GE	-	-	Galway, Waterford	diminitive of Baldwin	GE		-	-
(O)	Boey	IG	-	-	Cork, Donegal, Kilkenny	victorious	IG	(O)	Sullivan	IG
(O)	Bogue (Bowie)	IG	-	-	Cork, Kilkenny, Waterford	victorious	IG		Bowes	EN
	Bogue	SG	SC	-	Ulster	-	-		-	-

* see definitions

Prefix	Surname and Variation	Name Origin*	Migrated From*	Century Estab.	Geographical Locations	Definition of Surname	Language Origin*	Prefix	Pseudonyms and Synonyms	Name Origin*
(O)	Bohan(e) (Boughan, Buhan, Bohannen)	IG	-	-	Clark, Cork, Galway, Leitrim	victorious	IG		Bowen	WE
(O)	Boland	NS	-	-	Clare, Sligo	-	-		-	-
(O)	Bolger (Bulger)	IG	-	-	Wexford	belly, yellow	IG		-	-
	Bolton (Balton)	EN	EN	-	All Provinces	-	-		-	-
	Bonar	FR	GE	-	Limerick, Ulster	courteous	FR		-	-
	Bond	NF	EN	14th	All Provinces	unfree tenant	FR		-	-
	Booth	EN	EN	17th	Dublin, Sligo	cowman	EN		-	-
	Boughla (Bouhilly)	IG	-	-	Offaly	boy	IG		Buckley	EN
	Bourke	NF	EN	12th	All Provinces	-	-	Mac	David Philbin	IG NF
	Bourne	NF	EN	16th	Dublin, Kildare, Mayo	-	-		Burns Byron Byrne	SG EN IG
	Bowen	WE	EN	16th	Cork, Laois	-	-	(O) de	Bohane Bohun	IG NF
	Bowie	IG	-	-	Cork, Donegal, Kilkenny	-	-		-	-
	Bowler	NF	EN	-	Dublin, Kerry, Kildare, Louth, Meath	maker of bowls	NF		Fowler	EN
	Bowman	GE	-	-	Limerick, Ulster	-	-		-	-
	Boyce	NF	EN	-	Donegal	wood, shaft	NF	(O)	Bogue	IG
	Boyd	SG	SC	-	Ulster	yellow	SG		-	-

* see definitions

Prefix	Surname and Variation	Name Origin*	Migrated From*	Century Estab.	Geographical Locations	Definition of Surname	Language Origin*	Prefix	Pseudonyms and Synonyms	Name Origin*
(O)	Boylan	IG	-	-	Fermanagh, Louth, Monaghan	-	-		-	-
(O)	Boyle (Boylan)	IG	-	-	Kildare, Offaly	pledge	IG		Bohill	IG
(O)	Bracken	IG	-	-	Kildare, Offaly	speckled	IG		-	-
(O)	Bradden (Bredin, Breadon)	IG	-	-	Fermanagh, Tyrone	-	-		Salmon Fisher	EN EN
	Bradford	EN	EN	17th	Down	-	-		-	-
(O)	Bradigan (Bredican, Brodigan)	IG	-	-	Louth, Mayo, Meath, Roscommon, Sligo	spirited, urging	IG		-	-
	Bradley	EN	EN	-	Cork, Derry, Donegal, Tyrone	-	-		-	-
	Bradshaw	EN	EN	17th	Antrim, Down, Dublin, Tipperary	-	-		-	-
(Mac)	Brady	IG	-	-	Cavan, Clare	spirited, urging	-		-	-
(O)	Brallaghan	IG	-	-	Derry, Donegal, Tyrone	breast	IG		Bradley	EN
(O)	Braniff	IG	-	-	Down	raven, black	IG		-	-
(O)	Branigan (Brangan)	IG	-	-	Armagh, Monaghan	raven	IG		-	-
	Brannagh (Brennagh)	IG	-	-	Connacht	-	-		Walsh	IG
(Mac)	Brannan	IG	-	-	Roscommon	raven	IG		-	-
(O)	Brannan (Brennan)	IG	-	-	Fermanagh	raven	IG		-	-
(O)	Brawley (Brol(l)y)	IG	-	-	Derry	breast	IG		-	-

* see definitions

Prefix	Surname and Variation	Name Origin*	Migrated From*	Century Estab.	Geographical Locations	Definition of Surname	Language Origin*	Prefix	Pseudonyms and Synonyms	Name Origin*
	Bray (Bree)	IG	-	-	Meath, Munster, Wicklow	-	-		-	-
(O)	Brazil (Brassill)	IG	-	-	Waterford	strife	IG		-	-
(Mac)	Brearty (- Murty)	IG	-	-	Antrim, Donegal	son of Murtagh	IG		-	-
	Breadon	NF	EN	-	Leinster	-	-		-	-
	Breadon	IG	-	-	Ulster	-	-		-	-
(Mac)	Breen	IG	-	-	Kilkenny	sadness, sorrow	IG		-	-
(O)	Breen (Bruen)	IG	-	-	Offaly, Roscommon	sadness, sorrow	IG		-	-
(Mac)	Brehany (-Brehon)	IG	-	-	Sligo	-	-		Judge	EN
(O)	Brennan (Brannan)	IG	-	-	Fermanagh, Galway, Kerry, Kilkenny, Westmeath	sorrow	IG		-	-
	Brereton (Brerton)	NF	EN	16th	Tipperary	-	-		Bruton	EN
(O)	Breslin (Breslane)	IG	-	-	Donegal, Fermanagh, Sligo	strife	IG		Bryce Bryson	EN EN
	Brett (Britt)	FR	-	12th	Sligo, Tipperary, Waterford	breton	FR		Birt Burt Byrth	EN EN EN
(O)	Brick	IG	-	-	Galway, Kerry, Waterford	badger	IG		Badger	EN
Mac	Bride	IG	-	-	Donegal	devotee of St. Brigid	IG		-	-
Mac	Bride	SG	SC	-	Ulster	-	-		-	-
	Bridgeman	IG	-	-	Clare, Limerick	-	-		-	-

* see definitions

Prefix	Surname and Variation	Name Origin*	Migrated From*	Century Estab.	Geographical Locations	Definition of Surname	Language Origin*	Prefix	Pseudonyms and Synonyms	Name Origin*
	Bridgeman	EN	EN	17th	Cork	-	-		-	-
O'	Brien	IG	-	-	Clare, Limerick, Tipperary, Waterford	raven	IG		-	-
	Briscoe	EN	EN	16th	Cavan, Dublin, Sligo, Tipperary, Waterford	-	-		-	-
	Britton (Brittain)	FR	FR	-	Kildare, Meath, Tipperary, Waterford	derived from Brittany, France	FR		Brinton	EN
	Broder (Browder, Brodrick)	NS	-	-	Cork, Galway, Kilkenny	-	-		Brothers Broderick	EN EN
Mac	Brody	IG	-	-	Clare	-	-		-	-
(O)	Brogan	IG	-	-	Mayo	-	-		-	-
(O)	Brohan	IG	-	-	Offaly	corpulent	IG		Banks	EN
(O)	Brollaghan (Brallaghan)	IG	-	-	Cork, Derry, Donegal, Tyrone	breast	IG		-	-
(O)	Brolly (Brawley)	IG	-	-	Derry	breast	IG		-	-
	Brooke	EN	EN	16th	Ulster	-	-		-	-
(O)	Brophy	IG	-	-	Laois	-	-		-	-
(O)	Brosnan (Brosnahan, Bresnahan)	IG	-	-	Kerry	-	-		-	-
	Brothers	EN	EN	-	Cork, Galway, Kilkenny	-	-		-	-
	Broughall	IG	-	-	Leinster	-	-		-	-
	Browne	NF	EN	12th	Galway, Limerick	-	-		-	-
	Browne	EN	EN	-	Kerry, Mayo	-	-		-	-

* see definitions

Prefix	Surname and Variation	Name Origin*	Migrated From*	Century Estab.	Geographical Locations	Definition of Surname	Language Origin*	Prefix	Pseudonyms and Synonyms	Name Origin*
	Bruce	FR	SC	18th	Cork, Ulster	-	-		-	-
(O)	Bruen (Breen)	IG	-	-	Roscommon	-	-		Browne	NF
	Bryan	NF	EN	-	Kilkenny	-	-		-	-
	Bryson (Briceson)	EN	EN	-	Derry, Donegal	-	-		Price	WE
	Buchanan	SG	SC	-	Ulster	-	-		Mawhannon Bohan	IG IG
	Buckley (Buhilly, Boughla)	EN	EN	-	Cork, Offaly, Tipperary	-	-	(O)	Buhilly	IG
	Bunbury	EN	EN	17th	Carlow, Tipperary	-	-		-	-
	Bunyan (Bunion)	EN	EN	-	Kerry	-	-		Bennett Banane Binnane	FR IG IG
	Burke (deBurgh, Bourke)	NF	EN	12th	All Provinces	-	-		-	-
	Burnell	NF	EN	13th	Clare, Dublin, Meath	brown	NF		Bernal	NF
Mac	Burney (Birney)	NS	SC	-	Ulster	-	-		-	-
	Burns	SG	SC	-	Munster, Ulster	-	-	(O) (O) (O)	Beirne Birrane Byrne	IG IG IG
	Burnside	EN	EN	17th	Derry	-	-		-	-
	Burrows (Burris(s))	EN	EN	17th	Ulster	dweller at the bower house	EN		-	-
	Burton	EN	EN	-	Cork	-	-		-	-

* see definitions

Prefix	Surname and Variation	Name Origin*	Migrated From*	Century Estab.	Geographical Locations	Definition of Surname	Language Origin*	Prefix	Pseudonyms and Synonyms	Name Origin*
	Bury	NF	EN	13th	Ulster	-	-		Berry	EN
	Butler	NF	EN	-	Connacht, Leinster, Munster	-	-		-	-
	Byers	FR	SC	-	Armagh, Cavan	cowman	FR		-	-
(O)	Byrne	IG	-	-	Wicklow	raven	IG	Mac	Beirne Brinn Burns Byron Brien Bryan	IG IG SG EN IG NF
	Byron	EN	EN	-	Limerick, Tipperary	cowman	EN		-	-
Mac	Cabe (-Caba)	NS	SC	14th	Cavan, Leitrim, Meath Monaghan	cape or hood	NS		-	-
(O)	Cadane	IG	-	-	Ulster	-	-		-	-
	Caddell	WE	-	13th	Dublin, Galway	-	-		-	-
(O)	Cadogan (Cadigan)	IG	-	-	Cork	a blow or buffeted	IG		Blake	IG
	Cadogan	WE	-	13th	Dublin, Meath, Limerick	-	-		-	-
Mac	Caffery (-Caghery -Cahery)	IG	-	-	Fermanagh	equivalent to English Godfrey	IG	O'	Beatty Betty Caulfield	SG SG EN
(O)	Caghane	IG	-	-	Derry, Galway	-	-		-	-
Mac	Caghey	IG	-	-	Armagh, Kildare, Kilkenny, Tyrone	-	-		Hackett	NF
(O)	Cagney	IG	-	-	Cork	tribute or extraction	IG		-	-
(O)	Cahalane	IG	-	-	Cork, Kerry Limerick, Roscommon	battle mighty	IG		-	-

* see definitions

Prefix	Surname and Variation	Name Origin*	Migrated From*	Century Estab.	Geographical Locations	Definition of Surname	Language Origin*	Prefix	Pseudonyms and Synonyms	Name Origin*
(O)	Cahan (O'Kane Keane)	IG	-	-	Derry, Tyrone	-	-		-	-
(O)	Caherney	IG	-	-	Offaly	warlike	IG		Fox	EN
Mac	Cahill	IG	-	-	Cavan, Donegal	valor	IG	Mac	Charles Call	EN IG
(O)	Cahill	IG	-	-	Clare, Galway Kerry, Tipperary	valor	IG		Charles	EN
Mac	Cahon (Gahon)	IG	-	-	Ulster	-	-		-	-
Mac	Caig	IG	-	-	Galway	-	-		-	-
	Cain (Cane)	EN	EN	-	Derry, Mayo, Tyrone	-	-		-	-
	Cairns	SG	SC	-	Ulster	-	-		-	-
	Caldwell	EN	-	-	Cavan, Tyrone	-	-		Cardell Cardwell	EN EN
	Calhoun	SG	SC	-	Ulster	-	-		-	-
Mac	Call	IG	-	-	Armagh, Tyrone	-	-		Caulfield Cawell	EN IG
(O)	Callaghan (-Calligan)	IG	-	-	Clare, Cork	strife	IG		-	-
Mac	Callan	IG	-	-	Fermanagh	-	-		Collins	EN
(O)	Callan	IG	-	-	Armagh, Monaghan	-	-		-	-
(O)	Callaway	SG	SC	17th	Derry, Donegal	-	-		-	-
(O)	Callinan	IG	-	-	Galway, Kerry	-	-		-	-
Mac	Callion	SG	SC	-	Derry, Donegal	-	-	Mac	Allen	SG

* see definitions

Prefix	Surname and Variation	Name Origin*	Migrated From*	Century Estab.	Geographical Locations	Definition of Surname	Language Origin*	Prefix	Pseudonyms and Synonyms	Name Origin*
Mac	Callister (-Alister)	IG	SC	-	Antrim	-	-		-	-
	Callow	EN	EN	-	Leinster	bald	EN		-	-
Mac	Calmont (- Colman)	SG	SC	17th	Antrim	-	-		Dow	SG
(O)	Calnan (Callinan)	IG	-	-	Galway	-	-		-	-
Mac	Calvey (Calway)	IG	-	-	Mayo, Sligo	big headed	IG		Callow	EN
	Cambridge	EN	EN	-	Ulster	-	-		Chambers	NF
Mac	Cambridge	SG	SC	-	Ulster	-	-		-	-
	Cameron	SG	SC	-	Ulster	crooked nose	SG		-	-
Mac	Cammon	IG	-	-	Down	-	-		Hammond	EN
	Campbell	IG	-	-	Tyrone	battle chief	IG		Camp	EN
									Kemp	EN
								Mac	Cawell	IG
	Campbell	SG	SC	-	Cavan, Donegal	-	-		-	-
	Campion	NF	EN	17th	Kilkenny, Laois	combatant or champion-like	NF		-	-
(O)	Canavan	IG	-	-	Galway	-	-		Whitehead	EN
									White Lock	EN
Mac	Candless	IG	-	-	Ulster	-	-		-	-
Mac	Cann	IG	-	-	Armagh	wolf cub	IG		-	-
Mac	Canna	IG	-	-	Armagh, Clare Limerick	-	-		-	-
	Canning	EN	EN	17th	Derry	-	-		-	-

* see definitions

Prefix	Surname and Variation	Name Origin*	Migrated From*	Century Estab.	Geographical Locations	Definition of Surname	Language Origin*	Prefix	Pseudonyms and Synonyms	Name Origin*
	Canning	IG	-	-	Offaly, Westmeath	-	-		-	-
(O)	Cannon	IG	-	-	Donegal	wolf cub	IG		Canning	EN
Mac	Canny	IG	-	-	Clare, Tyrone	battle champion	IG		-	-
(O)	Canny	IG	-	-	Mayo	battle champion	IG		-	-
	Cantillion (Cantlin)	NF	EN	13th	Kerry	-	-		-	-
	Cantrell	EN	EN	17th	Dublin, Laois	-	-		-	-
(O)	Canty (County)	IG	-	-	Cork	satirical	IG		-	-
(O)	Caralane	IG	-	-	Derry	-	-		-	-
	Carbery	IG	-	-	Fermanagh, Waterford, Westmeath	-	-		-	-
	Cardell (Cardwell)	EN	EN	-	Down	-	-		-	-
	Carden	EN	EN	17th	Dublin, Mayo, Tipperary	-	-		-	-
	Cardiff (Kerdiff)	NF	WE	13th	Leinster	-	-		-	-
	Carew	NF	EN	-	Carlow, Cork, Mayo, Tipperary	-	-		Carey	EN
	Carey	EN	EN	13th	Cork, Donegal, Galway, Kerry, Tipperary	-	-		-	-
Mac	Carha	IG	-	-	Cork, Kerry	-	-		-	-
(O)	Carlan (d) (Carlin)	IG	-	-	Tyrone	-	-		-	-
	Carlisle	EN	EN	16th	Antrim	-	-		-	-

* see definitions

Prefix	Surname and Variation	Name Origin*	Migrated From*	Century Estab.	Geographical Locations	Definition of Surname	Language Origin*	Prefix	Pseudonyms and Synonyms	Name Origin*
	Carlton	EN	EN	-	Cavan, Derry, Meath, Tyrone	-	-		-	-
	Carmichael	SG	SC	-	Ulster	-	-		-	-
(O)	Carmody	IG	-	-	Clare	-	-		-	-
(O)	Carnahan	IG	-	-	Antrim, Armagh	-	-		-	-
Mac	Carney	IG	-	-	Meath, Ulster	victorious	IG		-	-
(O)	Carolan	IG	-	-	Cavan, Derry, Meath, Tyrone	-	-		-	-
	Carpenter	EN	EN	-	Armagh, Fermanagh	-	-		-	SG
	Carr	NF	EN	13th	All Provinces	man dear	IG		Kerr	EN
(Mac)	Carragher	IG	-	-	Armagh, Monaghan	hound, rock	IG		Rock	-
(Mac)	Carrig (Carrigy, Carraig, Carrick)	IG	-	-	Clare, Limerick, Tipperary	-	-		-	-
(Mac)	Carroll	IG	-	-	Leinster, Ulster	-	-		-	-
(O)	Carroll	IG	-	-	Armagh, Down, Fermanagh, Kerry, Kilkenny, Leitrim, Louth, Monaghan, Offaly	-	-		-	EN
(Mac)	Carron (-Carroon)	IG	-	-	Monaghan, Westmeath	calf	IG		Caulfield	EN
(Mac)	Carry	IG	-	-	Connacht, Ulster	-	-		Carr	-
	Carson	SG	SC	-	Ulster	-	-		-	-
(Mac)	Cart (-Art)	IG	-	-	Ulster	-	-		-	SG EN
(Mac)	Cartan	IG	-	-	Down	derived from forename Art	IG	Mac	Allen Carton	-
	Carter	EN	EN	14th	Limerick	-	-		-	

* see definitions

Prefix	Surname and Variation	Name Origin*	Migrated From*	Century Estab.	Geographical Locations	Definition of Surname	Language Origin*	Prefix	Pseudonyms and Synonyms	Name Origin*
Mac	Carthy	IG	-	-	Cork, Kerry	loving	IG	-	-	-
Mac	Cartney	SG	SC	-	Ulster	-	-	-	-	-
	Carton	EN	EN	17th	Ulster	-	-	-	-	-
(O)	Carty	IG	-	-	Connacht, Wexford	loving	IG	-	-	-
(Mac)	Carvey (Carway)	IG	-	-	Sligo	ragged	IG	-	-	-
Mac	Cary	IG	-	-	Galway, Westmeath	-	-	-	-	-
Mac	Casement	IG	-	-	Antrim	-	-	-	-	-
(Mac)	Casey	IG	-	-	Monaghan	watchful	IG	-	-	IG
(O)	Casey	IG	-	-	Cork, Dublin, Fermanagh, Mayo, Limerick, Roscommon	watchful	IG	(O)	Casse Keyes Keys	IG IG IG
	Cash (Cass, Casse)	IG	-	-	Dublin, Tipperary, Wexford	-	-	-	-	-
(Mac)	Cashin (Cashen)	IG	-	-	Kilkenny, Laois	bent, pleasant	IG	-	-	-
	Caskey (Mac Askie)	NS	-	-	Derry, Tyrone	-	-	-	-	-
(O)	Caslin (Cashlane)	IG	-	-	Leitrim, Roscommon	-	-	-	-	-
	Cass (Cash)	IG	-	-	Tippery, Wexford	-	-	-	-	-
(O)	Cassidy	IG	-	-	Leinster, Munster, Ulster	-	-	-	-	-
	Cather	NS	-	13th	Limerick, Tyrone	-	-	-	-	-
Mac	Caughan	IG	-	-	Antrim, Derry	-	-	Mac	Caghy	IG
(Mac)	Caugherty	IG	-	-	Down	-	-	Mac	Cartney	SG
Mac	Caughey (- Cahey)	IG	-	-	Tyrone	-	-	-	Mulcahy Hackett	IG NF

* see definitions

Prefix	Surname and Variation	Name Origin*	Migrated From*	Century Estab.	Geographical Locations	Definition of Surname	Language Origin*	Prefix	Pseudonyms and Synonyms	Name Origin*
	Caulfield	EN	EN	-	Ulster	-	-		-	-
Mac	Causland	SG	SC	17th	Derry, Tyrone	-	-		-	-
Mac	Cavana	IG	-	-	Antrim, Galway, Louth	monk	IG		-	-
	Cavendish	EN	EN	-	Connacht, Ulster	-	-		-	-
(Mac)	Cavish	IG	-	-	Cavan	-	-		Holmes Thompson Thomson	SG SG EN
(Mac)	Cavitt (- Kevitt)	IG	-	-	Galway, Louth, Ulster	-	-		-	-
Mac	Caw	IG	-	-	Antrim, Cavan	son of Adam	IG		-	-
Mac	Cawell	IG	-	-	Tyrone	battle chief	IG		-	-
Mac	Cawley (- Awley)	IG	-	-	Connacht, Fermanagh	-	-		-	-
	Chaff	EN	EN	-	Galway	chaff	EN		-	-
	Chamberlain	NF	EN	-	Cork	chamber (room)	NF		-	-
	Chamber (s)	NF	EN	-	Mayo, Ulster	of the chamber	NF		-	-
	Chaney	FR	-	-	Ulster	-	-		-	-
	Charleton (Charlton)	EN	EN	14th	Fermanagh, Sligo, Tyrone	-	-		-	-
	Charters (Chartres)	FR	-	17th	Cork, Ulster	maps, diagrams	FR		-	-
	Cheevers (Chivers)	FR	EN	12th	Wexford	goat	FR		-	-
	Cherry	EN	EN	17th	Ulster	-	-		-	-
(Mac)	Cheyne (Chesngy, Chesney, Chinnery, Chisholm, Chism)	NF	EN	16th	Down	oakgrove	NF		-	-

* see definitions

Prefix	Surname and Variation	Name Origin*	Migrated From*	Century Estab.	Geographical Locations	Definition of Surname	Language Origin*	Prefix	Pseudonyms and Synonyms	Name Origin*
	Christopher	IG	-	-	Waterford	-	-		-	-
	Christy	SG	SC	-	Ulster	-	-		-	-
	Church	EN	EN	17th	Ulster	-	-		-	-
(O)	Clabby	IG	-	-	Roscommon	wide-mouthed	IG		-	-
(Mac)	Claffey (- Clave)	IG	-	-	Ulster	lord or ruler	IG		Hand	EN
	Clancy	IG	-	-	Clare, Leitrim	-	-		-	-
(Mac)	Clarke	EN	EN	-	Cavan	-	-		-	-
(O)	Clavin (Clavan, Calveen)	IG	-	-	Laois, Offaly	a sick person	IG		Swords	IG
	Clay	EN	EN	-	Antrim	clay	EN		-	-
	Clayton	EN	EN	17th	All provinces	-	-		-	-
Mac	Clean (-Lean)	SG	SC	-	Antrim, Derry	form of John	SG		-	-
Mac	Cleary (- Aleary)	IG	-	-	Cavan, Sligo	clerk	IG		Clarke	EN
Mac	Clelland (- Cellan-Celand)	SG	SC	-	Sligo	-	-		-	-
	Clements	EN	EN	-	Donegal, Leitrim	possessing mantles	-		-	-
	Clements	SG	SC	-	Derry		-		Clements	EN
Mac	Clenaghan (- Lenahan)	IG	-	-	Antrim, Derry, Tyrone		IG		-	-
Mac	Clendinning	SG	SC	-	Antrim, Tyrone	-	-		-	-
(O)	Clerian	IG	-	-	Monaghan	clerk	-		-	-

* see definitions

Prefix	Surname and Variation	Name Origin*	Migrated From*	Century Estab.	Geographical Locations	Definition of Surname	Language Origin*	Prefix	Pseudonyms and Synonyms	Name Origin*
(O)	Clerihan	IG	-	-	Limerick	clerk	IG		-	-
(O)	Clery (Cleary)	IG	-	-	Donegal, Dublin, Munster	clerk	IG		Clarke	EN
(Mac)	Clifferty	IG	-	-	Tyrone	-	-		Clifford	EN
	Clifford	EN	EN	-	Ulster	-	-		-	-
Mac	Clintock	SG	SC	-	Antrim, Derry	refers to, St. Finian	SG		Lindsey	EN
	Clinton	EN	EN	-	Louth	-	-		-	-
Mac	Clinton	IG	-	-	Ulster	devotees of St. Finian	IG		Stone	EN
(O)	Clo(g)herty	IG	-	-	Galway	-	-		-	-
(O)	Clohessy	IG	-	-	Clare, Limerick	-	-		-	-
(O)	Cloney (Clooney, Clowney Clone)	IG	-	-	Down, Waterford	deceitful, flattering, rogue	IG		-	-
(O)	Cloonan (Cloney)	IG	-	-	Galway	deceitful, flattering, rogue	IG		-	-
Mac	Cloran	IG	-	-	Cavan, Galway	spokesman	IG		-	-
Mac	Clory (- Glory)	IG	-	-	Armagh, Down	spokesman	IG		-	-
	Close	EN IG	EN -	- -	Antrim	-	-		-	-
Mac	Closkey (- Cluskey)	IG	-	-	Derry	-	-		-	-
Mac	Cloud	SG	SC	-	Ulster	-	-		-	-
Mac	Cloughry	SG	SC	-	Donegal, Longford	stone, mason	-		Kingston	EN
Mac	Clown	IG	-	-	Clare	-	-		-	-

* see definitions

Prefix	Surname and Variation	Name Origin*	Migrated From*	Century Estab.	Geographical Locations	Definition of Surname	Language Origin*	Prefix	Pseudonyms and Synonyms	Name Origin*
Mac	Cloy	SG	SC	-	Antrim	-	-		-	-
(Mac)	Clune	IG	-	-	Clare	knee	IG		-	-
(Mac)	Clung (- Clurg)	SG	SC	-	Ulster	ship	SG		-	-
(Mac)	Clure	SG	SC	-	Ulster	-	-		-	-
(O)	Cluvane	IG	-	-	Kerry, Sligo	-	-		Clifford	EN
	Coakley	IG	-	-	Cork	-	-		-	-
Mac	Coan	IG	-	-	Armagh	-	-		Cowan	IG
	Coates (Cott)	EN	EN	14th	Antrim, Cork, Dublin, Tyrone	residnece at the cottage or sheep cote	EN		-	-
	Cobbe (Cob, Cobb)	EN	EN	17th	Dublin, Kildare Laois, Limerick, Offaly	derivative of Jacob	EN		-	-
	Cochrane	SG	SC	-	Ulster	-	-		-	-
	Codd	EN	EN	13th	Wexford	-	-		Codd	EN
	Cody	IG	-	-	Kilkenny	-	-		-	-
(O)	Coen (Cohen)	IG	-	-	Connacht	-	IG		-	-
	Coffey	IG	-	-	Cork, Galway, Meath Roscommon, Westmeath	victorious	IG		-	-
	Cogan (Coggan)	WE	EN	12th	Cork	-	-		Gogan Goggin	IG IG
(Mac)	Cogan	IG	-	-	Leitrim	hound, war	IG		-	-
	Cohen	JE	EE	-	Antrim, Down, Dublin	-	-		-	-
Mac	Coke	IG	-	-	Galway	-	-		-	-

* see definitions

Prefix	Surname and Variation	Name Origin*	Migrated From*	Century Estab.	Geographical Locations	Definition of Surname	Language Origin*	Prefix	Pseudonyms and Synonyms	Name Origin*
(Mac)	Colavin (Cullivan)	IG	-	-	Cavan, Connacht	-	-		Caldwell Colvin	EN EN
	Colbert	GE	EN	15th	Munster	-	-		-	-
Mac	Colgan (O'Colgan)	IG	-	-	Derry, Offaly	-	-		-	-
	Colhoun (Colquhoun)	SG	SC	-	Ulster	-	-		-	-
(O)	Colleran	IG	-	-	Galway, Mayo	-	-		-	-
	Collier (Colyer)	EN	EN	14th	Carlow, Kilkenny, Meath, Wexford	-	-		-	-
	Collins	EN	EN	-	Cork, Limerick, Ulster	-	-		-	-
	Collis	EN	EN	17th	Dublin, Kerry, Sligo	-	-		-	-
	Coleman	EN	EN	-	All provinces	-	-		-	-
(O)	Colman	IG	-	-	All provinces	dove	IG		Clifford Coleman	EN EN
(O)	Colter (Coulter)	IG	-	-	Down	-	-		-	-
Mac	Colum	IG	-	-	Longford, Ulster	dove	IG		-	-
	Colville	FR	SC	17th	Ulster	-	-		Coldwell Caldwell Colvin	EN EN EN
Mac	Combe (-Come, -Comish, Combs)	SG	SC	-	Armagh, Down	-	-		Holmes	SG
	Comber (Comer)	IG	-	-	Galway, Mayo	comb	IG		-	-
	Comerford	EN	EN	13th	Cavan, Kilkeny, Longford	-	-		-	-

* see definitions

Prefix	Surname and Variation	Name Origin*	Migrated From*	Century Estab.	Geographical Locations	Definition of Surname	Language Origin*	Prefix	Pseudonyms and Synonyms	Name Origin*
(Mac)	Comiskey (Cumisky)	IG	-	-	Cavan, Longford, Monaghan, Westmeath	confuser	IG		Comer / Comerford	IG / EN
(O)	Commane (Commons)	IG	-	-	Clare, Cork, Mayo, Wexford	-	-		Comyn / Hurley	NF / IG
	Comyn	NF	EN	-	Clare	-	-	(O)	Cummins / Comin / Comin / Cunningham / Conway	IG / IG / IG / SG / IG
(O)	Conaghan	IG	-	-	Derry, Donegal	-	-	Mac O	Cunningham	SG
Mac	Conaghy (- Conkey)	SG	SC	-	Ulster	son of Donagh	SG		-	-
(Mac)	Conamy (Conomy)	IG	-	-	Derry, Tyrone	hound of Meath	IG		Conway	IG
(Mac)	Conave	IG	-	-	Leitrim	expert swimmer	IG		Adams	EN
(O)	Conboy (Conaboy, Cunnaboy)	IG	-	-	Connacht	hound, yellow	IG		Conway	IG
(O)	Concannon	IG	-	-	Galway	hound, fair-hair	IG		-	-
	Condon	NF	EN	-	Cork	-	-		-	-
(O)	Condron (Conran)	IG	-	-	Fermanagh, Offaly	-	-		-	-
	Condy	FR	-	-	Tyrone	-	-		-	-
Mac	Cone	IG	-	-	Armagh	-	-		Cowan	IG
(Mac)	Conheeny	IG	-	-	Connacht	hound, fair, market	IG		Ford / Rabbitt	EN / EN
Mac	Conine	IG	-	-	Mayo	-	-		-	-

* see definitions

Prefix	Surname and Variation	Name Origin*	Migrated From*	Century Estab.	Geographical Locations	Definition of Surname	Language Origin*	Prefix	Pseudonyms and Synonyms	Name Origin*
(O)	Conlan	IG	-	-	All Provinces	-	-		-	-
(Mac)	Conlevy	IG	-	-	Longford	-	-		-	-
(Mac)	Conley (Conly)	IG	-	-	Offaly	-	-		-	-
Mac	Conn	IG	-	-	Down	-	-		-	-
(O)	Connachtan	IG	-	-	Derry, Donegal	-	-		-	-
(O)	Connaghty	IG	-	-	Cavan, Connacht	man from Connacht	IG		-	-
(O)	Connaughton	IG	-	-	Roscommon, Sligo	-	-		-	-
(Mac)	Conneely	IG	-	-	Galway	hound, valor	IG		-	-
(Mac)	Connell	IG	-	-	Antrim, Down, Tyrone	son of Daniel	IG		-	-
O'	Connell	IG	-	-	Kerry	son of Daniel	IG		-	-
(O)	Connellan (Conlan, Conlon)	IG	-	-	All Provinces	-	-		Kindelan Quinlan Quinlevan	IG IG IG
(O)	Connery	IG	-	-	Cork, Limerick	-	-		-	-
(Mac)	Connick	IG	-	-	Longford, Wexford	hound	IG		-	-
(O)	Connolly	IG	-	-	All Provinces	valorous	IG		-	-
(Mac)	Connon	IG	-	-	Monaghan	wolf cub	IG		-	-
Mac	Connor	IG	-	-	Ulster	son of Connor	-	Mac	Naugher	IG
O'	Connor	IG	-	-	Clare, Derry, Galway, Kerry, Offaly, Roscommon, Sligo	-	-		-	-
(O)	Conole	IG	-	-	Clare, Sligo	-	-		-	-
(O)	Conoo (Cunnoe)	IG	-	-	Cork, Offaly	head smashing	IG		Conway	IG

* see definitions

Prefix	Surname and Variation	Name Origin*	Migrated From*	Century Estab.	Geographical Locations	Definition of Surname	Language Origin*	Prefix	Pseudonyms and Synonyms	Name Origin*
(O)	Conrahy (Conroy)	IG	-	-	Laois, Offaly	-	-		-	-
(O)	Conroy (Conree, Conary, Conry)	IG	-	-	Clare, Galway, Roscommon	hound of prosperity	IG		King	EN
(Mac)	Considine	IG	-	-	Clare	-	-		-	-
Mac	Consnave	IG	-	-	Leitrim	-	-		-	-
Mac	Conville (- Conwell)	IG	-	-	Armagh, Down, Louth	-	-		-	-
Mac	Conway (Conboy, Convey, Mac Conaway)	IG	-	-	Clare, Limerick, Mayo Sligo, Tipperary, Tyrone	head smashing	IG		-	-
Mac	Conwell	IG	-	-	Donegal	-	-	Mac	Conville	IG
(O)	Coogan	IG	-	-	Galway, Kilkenny, Monaghan	-	-		Coggan Cogan	WE WE
	Cooke	EN	EN	-	Leinster	cook	EN		-	-
	Cooke (Mac Cooge, Mac Hugo)	IG	SC	-	Connacht	-	-		-	-
Mac	Cook (-Cuagh)	SG	-	-	Ulster	-	-		Cogan Cogan	WE WE
(Mac)	Cool	IG	-	-	Donegal	devotee of St. Comaghal	IG		Cole	EN
(O)	Coolahan	IG	-	-	Mayo	-	-		-	-
(O)	Cooley (Cowley, Colley)	IG	-	-	Clare, Galway, Ulster	-	-		-	-
(O)	Coonan (Conan)	IG	-	-	Offaly, Sligo, Tipperary	elegant	IG		-	-

* see definitions

Page 41

Prefix	Surname and Variation	Name Origin*	Migrated From*	Century Estab.	Geographical Locations	Definition of Surname	Language Origin*	Prefix	Pseudonyms and Synonyms	Name Origin*
(O)	Cooney (Coonan)	IG	-	-	Clare, Galway, Roscommon, Tyrone	elegant, handsome	IG		-	-
	Cooper	EN	EN	17th	Sligo	maker of tubs or vats	EN		-	-
	Coote	EN	EN	17th	Cavan, Laois	nickname from a bird	EN		-	-
	Coppinger	NS	-	14th	Cork	-	-		-	-
(O)	Corbane	IG	-	-	Connacht	-	-		Corbett	EN
	Corbett	EN	EN	-	Connacht, Munster	-	-		-	-
(Mac)	Corcoran	IG	-	-	Offaly	purple	IG		Cochrane	EN
(O)	Corcoran	IG	-	-	Fermanagh	purple	IG		Cochrane	EN
	Cordue	SP	-	-	Clare	-	-		-	-
	Corduff (Carduff)	IG	-	-	Donegal, Mayo	-	-		-	-
	Corish	IG	-	-	Connacht, Wexford	son of Piers	IG		-	-
Mac	Corkell (- Corkhill)	NS	SC	-	Derry, Donegal	-	-		-	-
(Mac)	Corless	IG	-	-	Galway	-	-		Charles	EN
Mac	Cormack (-Cormick)	SG IG	SC -	- -	Ulster Fermanagh, Longford	-	-		-	-
(O)	Comican (Mac Cormack)	IG	-	-	Clare, Down, Galway, Roscommon	-	-		-	-
Mac	Cormilla	IG	-	-	Monaghan	-	-	(O)	Gormley	IG
(O)	Corr	IG	-	-	Derry	spear	IG		-	-
(O)	Corrigan (Currigan, Courigan, Carrocan)	IG	-	-	Clare, Fermanagh, Tipperary	-	-		-	-

* see definitions

Prefix	Surname and Variation	Name Origin*	Migrated From*	Century Estab.	Geographical Locations	Definition of Surname	Language Origin*	Prefix	Pseudonyms and Synonyms	Name Origin*
(Mac)	Corry (Corrie, Corr)	IG	-	-	Fermanagh	Godfrey	IG		Weir	SG
	Cosby	EN	EN	16th	Laois	-	-		-	-
(Mac)	Cosgrave	IG	-	-	Monaghan	victorious	IG		Cosker	EN
(O)	Cosgrave (Cosgrove)	IG	-	-	Monaghan, Wicklow	victorious	IG		-	-
(Mac)	Costello(e)	NF	EN	-	Mayo	-	-		Costley	EN
(Mac)	Costigan	IG	-	-	Kickenny, Laois	derived from English name Roger	IG		-	-
Mac	Cotter	NS	-	-	Cork	-	-		-	-
	Cotton	EN	EN	17th	Dublin	-	-		-	-
(Mac)	Coughlan	IG	-	-	Offaly	cape or hood	IG		-	-
(O)	Coughlan (Coghlan)	IG	-	-	Cork	cape or hood	IG		-	-
de	Courcy	NF	EN	12th	Cork, Ulster	-	-		-	-
Mac	Court	IG	-	-	Armagh, Louth	-	-		Courtney	EN
	Courtney	NF	EN	-	Kerry	-	-		-	-
	Cowan	IG	-	-	Kilkenny, Ulster Waterford	-	-		Coen	IG
	Cowley	EN	EN	-	Kilkenny	-	-		-	-
(Mac)	Cowley (- Auley)	IG	-	-	Donegal	-	-		-	-
	Cowman (Mac Cowman)	IG	-	-	Wexford	-	-	(O)	Commons	IG
	Cowman	EN	EN	-	Dublin	-	-	(O)	Cummins	IG

* see definitions

Prefix	Surname and Variation	Name Origin*	Migrated From*	Century Estab.	Geographical Locations	Definition of Surname	Language Origin*	Prefix	Pseudonyms and Synonyms	Name Origin*
	Cox	EN	EN	-	Fermanagh, Monaghan, Roscommon	-	-	-	-	-
Mac	Coy	IG	-	-	Ulster	son of Hugh	IG	Mac	Kay	SG
Mac	Coyle	IG	-	-	Donegal, Monaghan	devotee of St. Comgal	IG		-	-
(O)	Coyne (Kilcone)	IG	-	-	Galway, Mayo	wild goose	IG	(O)	Barnacle Kyne Coen	EN IG IG
Mac	Cracken	SG	SC	16th	Antrim, Derry	the pure one	SG		-	-
	Craddock	WE	WE	13th	Kildare, Kilkenny, Meath	-	-		-	-
	Crahan	IG	-	-	Kerry, Leinster Mayo	-	-		-	-
	Craig	SG	SC	-	Antrim, Derry, Tyrone	crag, (steep, rugged rock)	SG		-	-
	Cramer	EN	EN	-	Armagh, Feremanagh,	creamer (peddler)	EN		-	-
	Cramer (Von Kramer)	GE	-	-	Cork	-	-		-	-
	Crampsey	IG	-	-	Donegal	-	-		Kneafsey	IG
	Crane	EN	EN	-	Kerry	bird	EN		-	-
(Mac)	Cranny	IG	-	-	Armagh, Down	-	-	Mac	Crany Creaney	IG IG
	Cravane (Creavan)	IG	-	-	Galway, Louth, Monaghan	-	-	Mac	Craven	EN
	Crawford	EN	EN	-	Antrim	-	-		-	-
Mac	Crea (- Crae, - Cray)	SG	SC	-	Ulster	-	-		-	-

* see definitions

Prefix	Surname and Variation	Name Origin*	Migrated From*	Century Estab.	Geographical Locations	Definition of Surname	Language Origin*	Prefix	Pseudonyms and Synonyms	Name Origin*
Mac	Cready (- Creedy, - Conready)	IG	-	-	Derry, Donegal	-	-		-	-
	Creagh	IG	-	-	Clare, Limerick	branch	IG		Creighton	SG
(O)	Creaghan	IC	-	-	Clare, Donegal, Galway, Sligo	-	-		Creighton	SG
	Creamer (Cramer, Traynor, Mac Creanor)	IG	-	-	Leitrim	-	-		-	-
(O)	Crean (Creaghan, Crehan)	IG	-	-	Clare, Donegal, Galway, Mayo, Sligo, Tyrone	heart	IG		Creighton Carey Crane	SG EN EN
Mac	Creary	IG	-	-	Tyrone	-	-		-	-
(O)	Creegan (Cregin)	IG	-	-	Connacht, Leinster, Munster	-	-		-	-
(O)	Creenan (Crinion)	IG	-	-	Laois, Kilkenny	old, worn out	IG		-	-
(O)	Crehan	IG	-	-	Mayo, Tyrone	-	-		-	-
(O)	Creighton	SG	SC	-	Ulster	-	-		-	-
(O)	Cremin (Cremeen)	IG	-	-	Munster	bent	IG		-	-
(Mac)	Crilly (O'Crilly)	IG	-	-	Derry	-	-		-	-
	Crofts	EN	EN	16th	Cork	croft	EN		-	-
Mac	Crohan	IG	-	-	Kerry	fox	IG		-	-
	Croke	EN	EN	13th	Tipperary	-	-		-	-
	Croker	NF	EN	13th	Kilkenny, Limerick	maker of pots	NF		-	-

* see definitions

Prefix	Surname and Variation	Name Origin*	Migrated From*	Century Estab.	Geographical Locations	Definition of Surname	Language Origin*	Prefix	Pseudonyms and Synonyms	Name Origin*
	Cromwell (Grummell)	EN	EN	15th	Limerick	-	-		-	-
(O)	Cronan	IG	-	-	Tipperary	brown or swarthy	SG		-	-
	Crooke	EN	EN	17th	Cork	a bend	EN		-	-
	Crooks	EN	EN	17th	Ulster	-	-		-	-
	Crosbie	EN	EN	17th	Kerry, Laois	-	-		-	-
(Mac)	Crossan	IG	-	-	Donegal, Laois, Offaly	cross	IG		Crosbie Cross	EN EN
(O)	Crotty	IG	-	-	Waterford	-	-		-	-
(O)	Crowley	IG	-	-	Cork, Roscommon	hard, hero	IG		-	-
(Mac)	Crowne (Croan)	IG	-	-	Roscommon	hound of Croghan	IG		-	-
	Crozier	EN	EN	-	Armagh, Fermanagh	-	-		-	-
	Cruise	NF	EN	-	Dublin, Meath	resident by the roadside or market cross	NF		-	-
(O)	Crumley (Cromley, Crumlish)	IG	-	-	Derry, Donegal	bent hero	IG		-	-
(Mac)	Crystal (Chrystal)	SG	SC	17th	Armagh, Tyrone	diminutive of Christopher	SG		-	-
(O)	Cuddigan (Cadogan)	IG	-	-	Cork	-	-		-	-
(O)	Cuddihy (Cuddy, Quiddihy)	IG	-	-	Cork, Kilkenny	helper	IG		-	-
Mac	Cue (Coo, - Hugh)	IG	-	-	Fermanagh	-	-		-	-

* see definitions

Prefix	Surname and Variation	Name Origin*	Migrated From*	Century Estab.	Geographical Locations	Definition of Surname	Language Origin*	Prefix	Pseudonyms and Synonyms	Name Origin*
(Mac)	Cuggerman	IG	-	-	Clare	whisper	IG		-	-
(O)	Culhane (Cohalan)	IG	-	-	Cork, Limerick	-	-		-	-
(O)	Culhoun (Culloon)	IG	-	-	Leinster, Ulster	-	-	(O)	Cullen	IG
Mac	Cullagh (- Collough)	IG	-	-	Ulster	hound of Ulster	IG		-	-
(O)	Cullane	IG	-	-	Cork, Limerick	whelp	IG		Collins	EN
Mac	Cullen (- Collin)	IG	-	-	Monaghan	holly	IG		Holly	EN
(O)	Cullen	IG	-	-	Kildare	holly	IG		-	-
(O)	Cullinan(e)	IG	-	-	Clare, Cork, Tipperary	holly	IG		Caldwell Quillinane Cullen	EN IG IG
(Mac)	Culreavy	IG	-	-	Leitrim, Longford	form of Charles, grey or brindled	IG		Gray	EN
(O)	Cumming(s) (Cummins, Commons)	IG	-	-	Clare, Cork, Mayo, Wexford	a hurley	IG		-	-
(O)	Cunnea (Conney)	IG	-	-	Ulster	-	-		Canning Rabbitt	EN EN
(Mac)	Cunneen (Cunnane)	IG	-	-	Connacht	wolf cub	IG		Rabbitt	EN
(O)	Cunneen	IG	-	-	Clare, Offaly	wolf cub	IG		Rabbitt	EN
Mac	Cunnegan	IG	-	-	Galway, Sligo	derived from personal name Conn.	IG		Cunningham	SG
(O)	Cunnegan	IG	-	-	Galway, Roscommon	derived from personal name Conn.	IG		Cunningham	SG

Prefix	Surname and Variation	Name Origin*	Migrated From*	Century Estab.	Geographical Locations	Definition of Surname	Language Origin*	Prefix	Pseudonyms and Synonyms	Name Origin*
(Mac)	Cunniff (Coneffe, Kinniff)	IG	-	-	Connacht, Cork, Leinster	hound, black	IG	-	-	-
	Cunningham	SG	SG	-	Ulster	-	-	(O)	Cunnegan	IG
(Mac)	Cuolahan	IG	-	-	Offaly	proud	IG	-	-	-
(O)	Cuolahan	IG	-	-	Mayo	proud	IG	-	-	-
(Mac)	Curley (Turley)	IG	-	-	Galway, Roscommon, Ulster	-	-	-	-	-
	Curphy (Murphy)	IG	-	-	Ulster	-	-	-	-	-
(O)	Curran (Currane)	IG	-	-	All Provinces	-	-	-	Carey, Crane	EN, EN
(Mac)	Curreen	IG	-	-	Leitrim	spear	IG	Mac, (O), (O)	Gurran, Curren, Crean	IG, IG, IG
(O)	Curreen	IG	-	-	Kerry, Waterford	spear	IG	(O), (O)	Carreen, Currin, Creen	IG, IG, IG
	Currie	SG	SC	-	Ulster	-	-	-	-	-
(O)	Curry (Corry)	IG	-	-	Clare, Limerick, Tipperary, Westmeath	-	-	-	-	-
(Mac)	Curtin	IG	-	-	Cork, Kerry, Limerick	hunchback	IG	-	-	-
	Curtis	NF	EN	13th	Leinster	well-educated man	NF	-	-	-
Mac	Cusack	NF	EN	12th	Meath	-	-	-	-	-
	Cusack	IG	-	-	Clare	-	-	-	-	-
(Mac)	Cushely (Cosgrave, Costello, Cuskley)	IG	-	-	Monaghan, Tyrone	-	-	-	-	-

* see definitions

Prefix	Surname and Variation	Name Origin*	Migrated From*	Century Estab.	Geographical Locations	Definition of Surname	Language Origin*	Prefix	Pseudonyms and Synonyms	Name Origin*
(O)	Cussane	IG	-	-	Galway	curly, path	IG		Patterson	EN
	Cussen (Cushing, Cushion)	NF	-	13th	Cork, Limerick, Tipperary, Wexford	cusin, kin	IG		Cousins	EN
(Mac)	Cutcheon (Hutchin, Hutchinson)	SG	SG	-	Ulster	diminutive of Hugh	SG		Houston Kitchen	SG EN
O'	Daa	IG	-	-	Clare, Tipperary	-	-		-	-
(O)	Daffy	IG	-	-	Clare	quarrelsome	IG		-	-
	Dagg	FR	EN	17th	Wexford, Wicklow	dagger	FR		-	-
Mac	Daid (- Davitt, - Divitt)	IG	-	-	Derry, Donegal	son of David	IG		Davison	SG
(O)	Dallaghan	IG	-	-	Connacht	blind	IG		-	-
	Dallas	SG	SC	-	Derry	dweller at the dalehouse	SG		Dalehouse	EN
	Dalton	NF	EN	-	Clare, Westmeath	-	-		-	-
(O)	Daly (Dawley, Dally)	IG	-	-	Clare, Cork, Galway, Westmeath	assembly	IG		-	-
	Dana(g)her	IG	-	-	Limerick, Tipperary	-	-		-	-
(O)	Dane	IG	-	-	Roscommon	dean	IG		-	-
(O)	Dane	EN	EN	-	Galway	valley	EN		-	-
	Darby	EN	EN	16th	Laois, Tipperary	-	-		-	-
	Darcy (Dorcey)	IG	-	-	Galway, Mayo, Wexford	dark	IG		-	-
	Darcy (O'Dorcy, D'Arcy)	NF	EN	-	Galway, Mayo, Meath, Wexford	dark	NF		-	-
	Dardis (D'Ardis)	NF	EN	-	Leinster	-	-		-	-

* see definitions

Prefix	Surname and Variation	Name Origin*	Migrated From*	Century Estab.	Geographical Locations	Definition of Surname	Language Origin*	Prefix	Pseudonyms and Synonyms	Name Origin*
(O)	Dargan (Dorgan)	IG	-	-	Cork, Leinster	red	IG		-	-
	Darley	EN	EN	17th	Dublin	-	-		-	-
(O)	Darmody (Dermody)	IG	-	-	Leinster, Tipperacy	-	-	Mac	Dermot	IG
(Mac)	Darragh (Darren, Darra)	IG	-	-	Antrim	oak	IG		Oakes	EN
	Daton (Daughton)	NF	EN	13th	Kilkenny	-	-		Dalton	NF
	Davenport	EN	EN	15\th	Dublin	-	-		-	-
	Davidson	SG	SC	-	Ulster	-	-		-	-
Mac	Davie (- Davy)	IG	-	-	Galway	-	-		Davie / Davis	IG / WE
(O)	Davin	IG	-	-	Tipperary	-	-		-	-
	Davis	WE	-	-	Cork	-	-		-	-
	Davitt (Mac Devitt)	IG	-	-	Mayo	-	-		-	-
(O)	Davoren	IG	-	-	Clare	black, two and Burren in Co. Clare	IG		-	-
	Dawson	EN	EN	17th	Monaghan, Tipperary	-	-		-	-
	Day	EN	EN	-	Clare	-	-		-	-
O'	Dea (Dee)	IG	-	-	Mayo, Tipperary	-	-		Day / Godwin	EN / EN
	Deane (Dane)	EN / IG / NF	EN / - / EN	-	Donegal, Galway, Kilkenny, Tipperary	-	-	(Mac)	Goodwin / Digney	EN / IG

* see definitions

Prefix	Surname and Variation	Name Origin*	Migrated From*	Century Estab.	Geographical Locations	Definition of Surname	Language Origin*	Prefix	Pseudonyms and Synonyms	Name Origin*
	Dease	NF	EN	13th	Meath	-	-		-	-
(O)	Deegan (Duigan)	IG	-	-	Laois	black, head	IG		Dickson	EN
(O)	Deehan	IG	-	-	Derry	-	-		Peoples	IG
(O)	Deeny	IG	-	-	Derry, Donegal	disagreeabe	IG		-	-
	Deering	EN	EN	16th	Laois	-	-		-	-
(O)	Delahunty (Dulanty)	IG	-	-	Offaly	plaintive, satirist	IG		-	EN
	Delahyde	NF	EN	13th	Dublin, Kildare, Meath	-	-	(O)	Hyde Skinnon	IG
	Delamer	NF	FR	-	Westmeath	-	-	Mac	Herbert	IG
(O)	Delaney (Delane)	IG	-	-	Kilkenny, Laois, Mayo	black	IG	(O)	Doolady	IG
	Deloughery (Deloorey, Dilloughery)	IG	-	-	Cork	black	IG		Dillworth	EN
(O)	Dempsey	IG	-	-	All Provinces	proud	IG		-	-
(O)	Dennehy	IG	-	-	Cork, Kerry	-	-		Denny	EN
(O)	Denning	IG	-	-	Cork	-	-		-	-
	Dennis	FR	-	-	Cork, Dublin	The Dane	FR	Mac	Donagh	IG
	Dennison	FR	-	-	Ulster	-	-	Mac	Donagh	IG
	Denny	EN	EN	16th	Derry	-	-		-	-
(O)	Demody (Darmody)	IG	-	-	Cavan, Galway, Kilkenny, Westmeath	-	-		-	-

* see definitions

Prefix	Surname and Variation	Name Origin*	Migrated From*	Century Estab.	Geographical Locations	Definition of Surname	Language Origin*	Prefix	Pseudonyms and Synonyms	Name Origin*
(O)	Dermond (Mac Dermot)	IG	-	-	Derry, Donegal	black troop	IG		Darby Dormer	EN FR
Mac	Dermot	IG	-	-	Roscommon	-	-		-	-
(O)	Derry	IG	-	-	Donegal	-	-		-	-
(O)	Desmond	IG	-	-	Cork	descendant of the Desmond man, south, Munster	-		-	-
(O)	Devanny (Devenny)	IG	-	-	Armagh, Connacht, Donegal	-	-		-	-
	Devereux	NF	EN	-	Wexford	-	-		Duvick Deverill Devery	NF NF NF
	Deverill (Devery)	NF	EN	-	Laois, Offaly	-	-		-	-
(O)	Devine (Devin, Davin)	IG	-	-	Louth, Meath	Poet	IG		-	-
(O)	Devlin (Dolan)	IG	-	-	Sligo, Tyrone	-	-		-	-
(O)	Devoy	IG	-	-	Laois	-	-		-	-
(O)	Diamond (Dimon[d])	IG	-	-	Connacht, Derry, Donegal	-	-		-	-
	Dick	SG	SC	17th	Antrim, Down	pet name for Richard	SG		Dix	EN
(O)	Diggin (Duigan, Deegan)	IG	-	-	Kerry	black, head	IG		-	-
(O)	Dillane	IG	-	-	Kerry, Limerick	-	-		Dillon	NF
	Dillon	NF	EN	-	Meath, Roscommon, Westmeath	-	-		-	-

* see definitions

Prefix	Surname and Variation	Name Origin*	Migrated From*	Century Estab.	Geographical Locations	Definition of Surname	Language Origin*	Prefix	Pseudonyms and Synonyms	Name Origin*
	Dillworth	EN	EN	-	Cork	-	-		-	-
(O)	Dinahan	IG	-	-	Limerick	-	-		-	-
(O)	Dinan (Dynan)	IG	-	-	Clare, Cork, Tipperary	-	-		-	-
(O)	Dinkin	IG	-	-	Connacht	brown head	IG		Duncan	SG
(O)	Dinneen	IG	-	-	Cork	brown	IG		Downing	EN
	Dinsmore (Dunsmore)	SG	SG	-	Derry, Donegal	-	-		-	-
	Disney	FR	FR	17th	Louth, Tipperary, Tyrone	-	-		-	-
(O)	Divine (Diveen)	IG	-	-	Derry, Tyron	black	IG		-	-
(O)	Diviney (Divenny)	IG	-	-	Mayo	black	IG		-	-
	Dobbin	EN	EN	14th	Antrim, Kilkenny, Waterford	diminutive of Robert	EN		-	-
	Dobbs	EN	EN	16th	Ulster	pet name of Robert	EN		-	-
(Mac)	Dockery	IG	-	-	Roscommon	hard	IG		Harden	EN
	Dodd	EN	EN	16th	Armagh, Down, Sligo	-	-		-	-
(O)	Doheny	IG	-	-	Cork	black	IG		Dawney	EN
(O)	Doherty (Doorty)	IG	-	-	Donegal	hurtful	IG		-	-
(O)	Dolan	IG	-	-	Cavan, Fermanagh, Galway, Leitrim, Roscommon	-	-	(O)	Doolin	IG
(O)	Dolly	IG	-	-	Galway	hero or champion, swift	-		-	-

* see definitions

Prefix	Surname and Variation	Name Origin*	Migrated From*	Century Estab.	Geographical Locations	Definition of Surname	Language Origin*	Prefix	Pseudonyms and Synonyms	Name Origin*
	Dolphin	NS	EN	12th	Galway	-	-		-	-
Mac	Donagh	IG	-	-	Cork, Sligo	son of Donagh	IG		-	-
Mac	Donald	SG	SC	-	Ulster	-	-		-	-
(O)	Donarty	IG	-	-	Tipperary	aggressive	IG		Davenport Dunworth Dunford Dunfort	EN EN EN EN
(O)	Donegan (MacDonegan)	IG	-	-	Cork, Monaghan, Offaly, Roscommon, Tipperary, Westmeath	black	IG		Dunnigan Dongan Duncan	IG EN SG
(Mac)	Donnell	IG	-	-	Antrim, Clare, Fermanagh	-	-	Mac	Donald	SG
O'	Donnell	IG	-	-	Clare, Donegal, Galway	-	-		-	-
(O)	Donnellan	IG	-	-	Galway, Offaly, Tyrone	diminutive of Donnell	IG		-	-
	Donnellson	SG	-	-	Antrim	-	-		Donaldson	SG
(O)	Donnnelly	IG	-	-	Tyrone	brown, valor	IG		-	-
(O)	Donoghue (Donohoe, Mac Doangh)	IG	-	-	Cavan, Cork, Galway, Kerry, Tipperary	son of Donagh	IG		-	-
(O)	Donovan	IG	-	-	Cork, Kilkenny, Limerick	black	IG		-	-
(O)	Doohan	IG	-	-	Clare, Donegal	-	-		-	-
(O)	Doolan	IG	-	-	Connacht, Leinster, Munster	challenger	IG	O	Dowling	IG
(O)	Dooley	IG	-	-	Offaly	black hero or champion	IG		-	-
(O)	Doonan	IG	-	-	Fermanagh, Leitrim, Roscommon	-	-	(O)	Donnan	IG

* see definitions

Prefix	Surname and Variation	Name Origin*	Migrated From*	Century Estab.	Geographical Locations	Definition of Surname	Language Origin*	Prefix	Pseudonyms and Synonyms	Name Origin*
(O)	Doonigan (Dunican)	IG	-	-	Fermanagh, Longford	-	-		-	-
(O)	Doran (Dorran)	IG	-	-	Laois, Westmeath	exiled person	IG		-	-
Mac	Dougal	SG	SC	-	Roscommon, Ulster	-	-	Mac	Dowell	IG
	Douglas	SG	SC	-	Ulster	-	-		-	-
	Dow	SG	SC	-	Ulster	dove, black	SG		-	-
O'	Dowd(a)	IG	-	-	Derry, Kerry, Sligo	black	IG	(O)	Dodd Doody	EN IG
Mac	Dowell	IG	-	-	Roscommon, Ulster	black, foreigner	IG	Mac (O)	Dougall Doyle	SG NS
(O)	Dowling	IG	-	-	Kerry, Laois	-	-		-	-
(O)	Downes	IG	-	-	Clare, Limerick	-	-		-	-
(O)	Downey	IG	-	-	Galway, Kerry	fort	IG		-	-
	Downing	EN	EN	-	Galway, Kerry	-	-		Dunning	EN
(O)	Downing	IG	-	-	Kerry	-	-		-	-
(O)	Doyle	NS	-	-	Leinster, Roscommon	black, foreigner	IG		-	-
(O)	Doyne	IG	-	-	Laois	-	-		Dunne Dynes	IG EN
	Drake	EN	EN	13th	Meath, Wexford	dragon	EN		-	-
	Draper	EN	EN	17th	Cork, Derry	-	-		-	-
	Drennan	IG	-	-	Galway	blackthorn	IG		Thornton	EN
(O)	Driscoll	IG	-	-	Cork	intermediary	IG		-	-
(O)	Dro(g)han	IG	-	-	Cork, Kilkenny, Waterford, Wexford	-	-		-	-

* see definitions

Prefix	Surname and Variation	Name Origin*	Migrated From*	Century Estab.	Geographical Locations	Definition of Surname	Language Origin*	Prefix	Pseudonyms and Synonyms	Name Origin*
(O)	Drum(m) (Drummy)	IG	-	-	Cavan, Cork, Fermanagh	ridge	IG		Drummond	SG
	Duff	IG	-	-	Tyrone, Waterford	black	IG		Black	EN
Mac	Duff	SG	SG	-	Ulster	-	-		-	-
(O)	Duffy	IG	-	-	Donegal, Monaghan, Roscommon	black, head	IG		-	-
(O)	Dug[g]an (Doogan, Dougan)	IG	-	-	Cork, Galway, Mayo, Ulster	black	IG		-	-
	Duke	FR	FR	16th	Connacht, Ulster	leader	FR		-	-
	Dunbar	SG	SC	17th	Donegal, Fermanagh	-	-		-	-
	Duncan	SG	SC	-	Ulster	-	-		-	-
(O)	Dunlea	IG	-	-	Cork	brown	IG		-	-
(Mac)	Dunlevy	IG	-	-	Donegal, Down	mountain	IG		Dunlief Dunlop	SG SG
(O)	Dunn[e] (O'Doyne)	IG	-	-	Laois	brown	IG		-	-
(O)	Dunphy (Dunfy)	IG	-	-	Kilkenny	-	-		-	-
	Durham (Derham)	EN	EN	14th	Cock, Derry, Dublin	-	-		-	-
(Mac)	Durkan (Dorcan, Dorkin)	IG	-	-	Sligo	pessimist	IG		Gurkin Zorkin	IG IG
(O)	Durnin (Durnian)	IG	-	-	Louth, Ulster	fist	IG		Durning	EN
(O)	Dwayne (Divane, Duane, Devane, Downes)	IG	-	-	Connacht, Munster	-	-		-	-

* see definitions

Prefix	Surname and Variation	Name Origin*	Migrated From*	Century Estab.	Geographical Locations	Definition of Surname	Language Origin*	Prefix	Pseudonyms and Synonyms	Name Origin*
(O)	Dwyer	IG	-	-	Tipperary	dun-colored	IG		Dyer	EN
	Dyer	EN	EN	-	Roscommon, Sligo	-	-		-	-
Mac	Dyer (-Dwyer)	IG	-	-	Donegal	black	IG		-	-
	Dynes (Dyne)	FR	EN	-	Ulster	-	-		-	-
	Eagar	EN	EN	17th	Down, Kerry	derived from the name of Edgar	EN		Eager	EN
	Eames	EN	EN	17th	All provinces	uncle	EN		Agar	EN
	Early	IG	-	-	Cavan, Leitrim	early rising	IG		-	-
	Eastwood	EN	EN	17th	Dublin, Louth, Ulster	-	-		-	-
	Eaton	EN	EN	16th	Leinster, Ulster	-	-		-	-
	Edwards	EN	EN	-	Antrim, Dublin, Wexford	-	-		-	-
(Mac)	Egan	IG	-	-	Galway, Tipperary	son of Egan	IG		-	-
Mac	Egoe	SP	SP	-	Roscommon	a spanish form of James	SP		-	-
	Elder	EN	EN	-	Derry, Donegal	senior	EN		-	-
Mac	Elderry	IG	-	-	Antrim, Tyrone	dark	IG		-	-
Mac	Eldowney (-Gildowney)	IG	-	-	Derry, Down	son of the devotee of the church	IG		-	-
Mac	Elhair (Kilcarr)	IG	-	-	Donegal	devotee of St. Cathair	IG		Carr	EN
Mac	Elheney	IG	-	-	Donegal, Down, Leitrim, Roscommon	-	-		-	-

* see definitions

Prefix	Surname and Variation	Name Origin*	Migrated From*	Century Estab.	Geographical Locations	Definition of Surname	Language Origin*	Prefix	Pseudonyms and Synonyms	Name Origin*
Mac	Elheron (-Leheron)	IG	-	-	Ulster	devotee of St. Kieran	IG		-	-
Mac	Ellen	IG	-	-	Armagh	-	-		-	-
Mac	Elligott (Fitzelias)	NF	EN	13th	Kerry	-	-		-	-
	Elliott	EN	EN	16th	Ulster	-	-		-	-
	Ellis (Elias, Elys)	EN	EN	13th	Dublin, Ulster	-	-		-	-
	Ellison	EN	EN	17th	Dublin	-	-		-	-
Mac	Elmeel	IG	-	-	Monaghan	devotee of St. Michael, bald	IG		-	-
	Elmore (Elmer)	EN	EN	17th	Louth	-	-		-	-
Mac	Elmoyle	IG	-	-	Antrim, Derry	devotee of St. Michael, bald	IG		-	-
Mac	Elmurray (Murray, Kilmary)	IG	-	-	Derry, Fermanagh, Tyrone	devotee of the blessed Virgin Mary	IG		-	-
Mac	Elnay	IG	-	-	Monaghan	of the saints	IG		Ford	EN
Mac	Elroy (Gilroy, Kilroy)	IG	-	-	Connacht, Fermanagh	red-haired youth	IG		-	-
Mac	Elwee (-Gilloway)	IG	-	-	Derry, Donegal	yellow, fellow or youth	IG		Gilbey	EN
	Emerson	EN	EN	-	Ulster	-	-		-	-
	Emmet	EN	EN	17th	Dublin, Tipperary	derived from female name of Emma	EN		-	-
	Emo (Emor)	EN	EN	-	Cavan, Fermanagh	-	-		-	-

* see definitions

Prefix	Surname and Variation	Name Origin*	Migrated From*	Century Estab.	Geographical Locations	Definition of Surname	Language Origin*	Prefix	Pseudonyms and Synonyms	Name Origin*
Mac	Ena	IG	-	-	Carlow, Wexford	-	-		-	-
(O)	Encantie	IG	-	-	Cork	-	-		-	-
Mac	Enarie	IG	-	-	All Provinces	-	-		-	-
Mac	Enchroe	IG	-	-	Clare, Limerick, Tipperary, Ulster	-	-		Crowe	EN
Mac	Eneany	IG	-	-	Armagh, Down, Fermanagh, Louth, Monaghan, Roscommon	dean	IG		Bird Rabbitt	EN EN
Mac	Enery (-Eniry, -Henry, Henry)	IG	-	-	Limerick	easily roused, early	IG		-	-
	England	NF	EN	-	Cork	-	-		-	-
	English (l'Angleis)	NF	EN	13th	Limerick	The Englishman	NF		England	EN
	Ennis (Ennos, Enos)	IG	-	-	Meath, Westmeath	descendant of Angus	IG		-	-
(Mac)	Enright (Enraghty)	IG	-	-	Claire, Limerick	attack	IG		-	-
Mac	Enroe (Roe)	IG	-	-	Cavan, Leitrim	-	-		Roe Rowe	EN EN
Mac	Entaggart (-Taggart, Tiger)	IG	-	-	Fermanagh	priest	IG		-	-
Mac	Entee	IG	-	-	Armagh, Monaghan	scholar	IG	Mac Mac	Atee Ginty	IG IG
Mac	Entosh (-Intosh)	SG	SC	-	Ulster	son of the chieftain	SG		-	-
	Ercke	IG	-	-	Tyrone	devotee of St. Eric	IG		Herrick	EN

* see definitions

Prefix	Surname and Variation	Name Origin*	Migrated From*	Century Estab.	Geographical Locations	Definition of Surname	Language Origin*	Prefix	Pseudonyms and Synonyms	Name Origin*
Mac	Erlean	IG	-	-	Derry, Sligo	learned man	IG		-	-
	Esmond	EN	EN	12th	Wexford	favor protection	EN		-	-
	Etchingham (Itchingham)	EN	EN	16th	Wexford	-	-		-	-
Mac	Ettigan (Gettigan)	IG	-	-	Donegal, Tyrone	-	-		-	-
	Eustace	NF	EN	-	Kildare	fruitful	GR		-	-
Mac	Evanny	IG	-	-	Mayo	monk	IG		Monks	EN
	Evans	WE	-	-	Kilkenny, Tipperary	swift	WE		-	-
	Evers	NF	EN	14th	Meath, Munster	-	-		Ivers	EN
Mac	Evilly	IG	-	-	Mayo	worrior or knight	IG		-	-
Mac	Evinney (- Avinney)	IG	-	-	Derry, Fermanagh	-	-		-	-
Mac	Evoy (- Avoy)	IG	-	-	Laois, Wexford	woodman	IG	Mac Mac	Veagh Avay	IG IG
	Ewing	SG	SC	17th	Ulster	well-born	GR		-	-
	Eyre (Ayres)	EN	EN	16th	Galway	heir	EN		-	-
Mac	Fadden (- Fadyen)	IG	-	-	Donegal, Mayo	diminitive form of Padraig (Patrick)	IG		-	-
Mac	Fadden	SG	-	-	Ulster	-	-		-	-
	Fagan	NF	EN	-	Dublin, Meath	-	-		-	-
	Fagan	IG	-	-	Armagh, Down, Fermanagh, Louth, Monaghan	-	-		-	-

* see definitions

Prefix	Surname and Variation	Name Origin*	Migrated From*	Century Estab.	Geographical Locations	Definition of Surname	Language Origin*	Prefix	Pseudonyms and Synonyms	Name Origin*
(O)	Faherty	IG	-	-	Galway	-	-	(O)	Flaherty	IG
(O)	Fahy (Faghy)	IG	-	-	Galway	lawn or green	IG		Green, Fay	EN, EN
(O)	Fairy	IG	-	-	Connacht, Donegal	manly, king	IG		Feary	EN
	Falkiner (Falconer)	EN	EN	-	Ulster	-	-		-	-
Mac	Fall	SG	SC	-	Ulster	-	-		-	-
(O)	Fallaher	IG	-	-	Clare, Tipperary	wolf dear	IG		-	-
(O)	Fallon (Falloon)	IG	-	-	Armagh, Down, Roscommon, Tryone	ruler	IG		Folan	IG
	Falls	EN	EN	17th	Tyrone	-	-		-	-
(O)	Falsey (Falahee)	IG	-	-	Clare	wolf	IG	Mac	Phail, Lavelle	IG, IG
(O)	Falvey	IG	-	-	Clare, Cork, Kerry	lively	IG		-	-
	Fanning (Fannin)	NF	EN	-	Limerick, Tipperary	-	-		Fealy	IG
Mac	Farland	IG	-	-	Armagh, Tyrone	-	-		-	-
	Farley	EN	EN	-	Cavan	-	-		-	-
	Farlow	EN	EN	17th	LImerick	-	-		-	-
	Farmer	EN	EN	-	Fermanagh, Monaghan	-	-		-	-
	Farnham (Farneham)	EN	EN	-	Tyrone, Waterford	-	-		Farnham	-
(O)	Farnon (Farnan)	IG	-	-	Tyrone	-	-			EN

Prefix	Surname and Variation	Name Origin*	Migrated From*	Century Estab.	Geographical Locations	Definition of Surname	Language Origin*	Prefix	Pseudonyms and Synonyms	Name Origin*
(O)	Farrell (Ferrall)	IG	-	-	All Provinces	man of valor	IG		-	-
(O)	Farrelly (Farrel)	IG	-	-	Cavan	man of valor	IG		Farley	EN
(O)	Farren	IG	-	-	Donegal	-	-		-	-
	Farrington	EN	EN	14th	Ulster	-	-		-	-
(O)	Farris	IG	-	-	Cavan, Donegal, Leitrim	man, action	IG		-	-
(O)	Farrissy	IG	-	-	Leitrim, Mayo	man, action	IG		-	-
	Faulkner (Faulkney)	IG	-	-	Mayo	-	-		Falinker Falconer	EN EN
(O)	Faughan	IG	-	-	Leitrim, Longford	-	-		-	-
	Fawcett (Fossitt)	EN	EN	16th	All Provinces	-	-		-	-
	Fay	NF	EN	12th	Cavan, Monaghan, Meath, Westmeath	-	-		Green	EN
	Fealy	IG	-	-	Kerry	-	-		-	-
(O)	Fearon (Feran)	IG	-	-	Ulster	man	IG	(O)	Farron	IG
(O)	Fee (Fey, Foy, Fye)	IG	-	-	Armagh, Cavan, Connacht, Fermanagh	raven, hunt	IG		Fay Hunt	NF EN
(O)	Feehan	IG	-	-	Kilkenny, Tipperary	raven, hunt	IG		Fane	EN
(Mac)	Feely (Fehilly)	IG	-	-	Derry, Donegal	chess player	IG		Field	EN
(O)	Feeney	IG	-	-	Galway, Roscommon, Sligo	soldier	IG		-	-

* see definitions

Page 62

Prefix	Surname and Variation	Name Origin*	Migrated From*	Century Estab.	Geographical Locations	Definition of Surname	Language Origin*	Prefix	Pseudonyms and Synonyms	Name Origin*
(O)	Fehilly	IG	-	-	Connacht, Cork	chess player	IG	(Mac)	Feely Field	IG EN
(O)	Feighney (Feheny)	IG	-	-	Roscommon	raven, hunt	IG		Hunt	EN
(O)	Feighry (Feery)	IG	-	-	Tyrone	-	-		Hunt	EN
(O)	Fen(e)lon	IG	-	-	Westmeath	fair	IG		-	-
	Fenelon	FR	FR	-	Westmeath	-	-		-	-
(O)	Fennell	IG	-	-	Clare, Dublin, Kilkenny, Tipperary	fair, valor	IG		-	-
	Fennell	EN	EN	14th	Kilkenny, Tipperary	-	-		-	-
(O)	Fennelly	IG	-	-	Kilkenny, Laois, Offaly	fair, valor	IG		-	-
	Fenner (Fennors, Finure)	NF	EN	14th	Dublin, Kilkenny	-	-		Finley Fanning	SG NF
(O)	Fergus	IG	-	-	Kerry, Leitrim, Mayo	man, vigour	IG		-	-
	Ferguson	SG	SC	-	Leitrim, Ulster	-	-		Fennerty Ferguson Ferris	IG SG -
Mac	Ferran	IG	-	-	Antrim, Down, Roscommon	swift	IG		-	-
(O)	Ferrigan	IG	-	-	Down, Louth	anger, manikan	IG		-	-
	Ferris	SG	SC	-	Ulster	-	-		-	-
	Ferris	IG	-	-	Kerry	-	-		-	-
	Feriter	EN	EN	13th	Kerry	hunt, search	EN		-	-
	Featherston	EN	EN	17th	Roscommon, Westmeath	-	-		-	-

* see definitions

Prefix	Surname and Variation	Name Origin*	Migrated From*	Century Estab.	Geographical Locations	Definition of Surname	Language Origin*	Prefix	Pseudonyms and Synonyms	Name Origin*
Mac	Fettridge	IG	-	-	Antrim	son of Petrus	IG		-	-
	Fields (Fielding)	EN	EN	-	Connacht, Cork	-	-		-	-
	Figgis	FR	EN	-	Antrim, Down, Dublin	faithful	FR		-	-
(O)	Finaghty	IG	-	-	Roscommon	snow	IG		Fenton	EN
	Finch	EN	EN	17th	Munster, Ulster	nickname from the bird	EN		-	-
	Finlay (Findley)	SG	SC	-	Laois, Offaly	-	-		-	-
(O)	Finn	IG	-	-	Galway, Monaghan, Munster, Sligo	-	-		-	-
	Finnamore	FR	-	13th	Leinster	dear love	FR		-	-
(O)	Finnegan (Finegan)	IG	-	-	Galway, Roscommon, Ulster	-	-		-	-
(Mac)	Finucane (Kinucane)	IG	-	-	Clare	son, fair	IG		-	-
Mac	Firbis	IG	-	-	Connacht	man of property	IG		Forbes	SG
	Fisher	EN	EN	-	Ulster	-	-		-	-
	Fitzandrew	NF	EN	17th	Mayo	son of Andrew	NF		-	-
	Fitzelle	NF	EN	12th	Antrim, Kerry	-	-		Fizelle	GE
	Fitzeustace	NF	EN	-	Carlow, Kildare	son of Eustace	NF		-	-
	Fitzgerald	NF	NR*	-	Cork, Kerry, Kildare, Limerick	son of Gerald	NF		Garrett	EN
	Fitzgibbon	NF	-	-	Limerick, Mayo	son of Gibbon	NF		-	-
	Fitzharris	NF	-	-	Wexford	son of Harris	NF		Fitzhenry	NF

* see definitions

Prefix	Surname and Variation	Name Origin*	Migrated From*	Century Estab.	Geographical Locations	Definition of Surname	Language Origin*	Prefix	Pseudonyms and Synonyms	Name Origin*
	Fitzhenry	NF	EN	-	Connacht	son of Henry	NF		Henry	IG
	Fitzherbert	NF	EN	-	Kerry, Westmeath	son of Herbert	NF		-	-
	Fitzjames	NF	EN	-	Carlow, Wicklow	son of James	NF		James	EN
	Fitzmartin	NF	EN	-	Tyrone	son of Martin	NF		-	-
	Fitzmaurice	NF	EN	-	Kerry, Mayo	son of Maurice	NF		Morris Morris	NF IG
	Fitzpatrick	IG	-	-	Fermanagh, Laois	devotee of St. Patrick	IG		-	-
	Fitzsimon(s) (Fitzsimmons)	NF	EN	14th	Cavan, Down, Mayo, Westmeath	son of Simon	NF	Mac	Eddery	IG
	Fitzstephens	NF	EN	-	Ulster	son of Stephen	NF		Stephens Stevenson Sliney	IG EN IG
	Fitzwalter	NF	EN	-	Clare, Cork, Kerry, Waterford	son of Walter	NF	Mac	-	-
	Fitzwilliam	NF	EN	-	Leinster	son of William	NF		-	-
	Flack (Fleck)	SG	SG	-	Ulster	-	-		-	-
(O)	Flahavan (Flavahan)	IG	-	-	Cork, Waterford	ruler	IG		-	-
(O)	Flaherty (Flaverty)	IG	-	-	Connacht, Galway, Kerry	bright ruler	IG		-	-
(O)	Flanagan	IG	-	-	Fermanagh, Offaly, Roscommon	red or ruddy	IG		-	-
(O)	Flannery	IG	-	-	Limerick, Mayo	red or ruddy, eyebrow	IG		-	-

* see definitions

Prefix	Surname and Variation	Name Origin*	Migrated From*	Century Estab.	Geographical Locations	Definition of Surname	Language Origin*	Prefix	Pseudonyms and Synonyms	Name Origin*
(O)	Flatley	IG	-	-	Sligo	prince, poet	IG		-	-
(O)	Flattery	IG	-	-	Offaly	-	-		-	-
(O)	Flavey	IG	-	-	Clare, Cork, Kerry	lively	IG		-	-
	Fleming	NF	NE	12th	All Provinces	a man from Flanders	NF		-	-
	Fletcher	SG	SC	-	Ulster	-	-		-	-
	Flood (Floody)	EN	EN	13th	Leinster, Ulster	-	-		Flood	EN
	Floyd (Lloyd)	WE	-	-	Munster	grey	WE		-	-
(O)	Flynn (Flying)	IG	-	-	Clare, Cork, Kerry, Roscommon, Ulster	ruddy, red	IG		-	-
(O)	Fogarty	IG	-	-	Tipperary	expelling, banished	IG		-	-
(O)	Folan(e)	IG	-	-	Galway, Mayo	-	-		-	-
(O)	Foley	IG	-	-	Munster	plunderer	IG		Sharry	IG
	Folliot	FR	-	15th	Donegal, Dublin	gay	FR		-	-
(O)	Foody (Foudy)	IG	-	-	Mayo	plundering	IG	Mac	Speed Swift	EN EN
(O)	Foohy	IG	-	-	Cork	-	-		-	-
(O)	Foran	IG	-	-	Limerick, Waterford	-	-		Ford	EN
	Forbes	SG	SC	-	Clare, Longford	-	-		-	-
(O)	Ford(e)	EN	EN	-	Galway, Leitrim	-	-		-	-
	Forhane	IG	-	-	Cork, Kerry	-	-		Ford	EN
	Forkin (Forkan)	IG	-	-	Galway, Mayo	fork	IG		Goulding	EN

* see definitions

Prefix	Surname and Variation	Name Origin*	Migrated From*	Century Estab.	Geographical Locations	Definition of Surname	Language Origin*	Prefix	Pseudonyms and Synonyms	Name Origin*
	For(r)estal	NF	EN	-	Kilkenny	paddock	NR		-	-
	Forsythe (Foursides)	SG	SC	-	Antrim, Down	man of peace	SG		-	-
(O)	Fortune (Fortin, Forty)	IG	-	-	Carlow, Cork, Wexford	overlord	IG		Fortune	EN
	Fowloo	EN	EN	17th	Ulster	-	-		Fowler	EN
	Fowler	EN	EN	17th	Ulster	-	-			
	Fox	EN	EN	-	Limerick, Offaly	-	-		-	-
(O)	Foy	IG	-	-	Armagh, Cavan, Fermanagh	raven, hunt	IG		-	-
	Foyle	FR	-	13th	Dublin, Laois	excavation	FR		-	-
(O)	Fraher (Farraher)	IG	-	-	Galway, Mayo, Waterford	man dear	IG		-	-
	Francis	NF	EN	-	Galway	The Frenchman	NF		-	-
	Franklin	EN	EN	17th	Limerick, Tipperary	freeholder	EN		-	-
	Franks	EN	EN	17th	Laois, Offaly	Frenchman	EN		-	-
(O)	Frawley	IG	-	-	Clare, Limerick	-	-		-	-
	Frazier (Fraser)	SG	SC	-	Ulster	-	-	Mac	Frizell, Barron	NF, IG
	Freeborne (Frebern)	EN	EN	17th	Donegal, Wexford	free born	EN		-	-
	Freeney	NF	EN	15th	Kilkenny, Waterford	of the ash	NF		-	-
	Fridberg	JE	EE	-	Dublin	-	-		-	-
(O)	Friel	IG	-	-	Donegal	-	-		-	-

* see definitions

Prefix	Surname and Variation	Name Origin*	Migrated From*	Century Estab.	Geographical Locations	Definition of Surname	Language Origin*	Prefix	Pseudonyms and Synonyms	Name Origin*
	Frizell	NF	EN	13th	Munster	-	-		-	-
	Frost	EN	EN	18th	Clare	-	-		-	-
	Fuller	EN	EN	16th	Down, Kerry	-	-		-	-
	Fulton	SG	SC	17th	Ulster	-	-		-	-
(O)	Furey	IG	-	-	Galway, Westmeath	-	-		Fleury	IG
	Furlong	EN	EN	13th	Wexford	-	-		-	-
(O)	Furphy	IG	-	-	Armagh, Tyrone	perfect	IG		-	-
	Gaffney	IG	-	-	Cavan, Donegal, Galway, Roscommon, Tyrone	-	-		Caulfield	EN
(O)	Gahan	IG	-	-	Wexford, Wicklon	wind	IG		Hackett	NF
Mac	Gahey	IG	-	-	Monaghan	-	-		Hackett	NF
	Galbraith	SG	SC	17th	Fermanagh, Galway, Laois, Tyrone	Welshman	SG		-	-
(O)	Gallagher	IG	-	-	Donegal	foreign help	IG		-	-
(O)	Gallen	IG	-	-	Donegal	-	-		-	-
(Mac)	Gallery	IG	-	-	Clare	brindled	IG		-	-
(O)	Galligan (Gilligan)	IG	-	-	Cavan, Sligo	white	IG		White	EN
(Mac)	Gallogly (Gologly)	IG	-	-	Antrim, Donegal, Monaghan	galloglass (mercenary, usually Scottish)	IG		English Englishby Golightly	NF EN EN
(O)	Galvin (Galvan, Gallvan)	IG	-	-	Clare, Kerry	bright, white	IG		-	-

* see definitions

Prefix	Surname and Variation	Name Origin*	Migrated From*	Century Estab.	Geographical Locations	Definition of Surname	Language Origin*	Prefix	Pseudonyms and Synonyms	Name Origin*
	Galwey (Gallwey)	IG	-	-	Cork	-	-		Galloway	SG
	Galwey	SG	SC	-	Ulster	-	-		-	-
Mac	Gamble (Gammell)	SW	-	17th	Cork, Ulster	old	SW		-	-
	Gambon	FR	-	-	Waterford	leg	FR		Legge	EN
(Mac)	Gammon	IG	-	-	Clare	-	-		Gambon	FR
O'	Gannon	IG	-	-	Clare, Mayo	fair	IG		-	-
	Gara	IG	-	-	Mayo, Sligo	dog	IG		-	-
	Garland (Gernon)	NF	EN	12th	Louth, Monaghan	-	-		-	-
	Garrett	EN	EN	-	Ulster	-	-		-	-
(Mac)	Garrigan (Gargan)	IG	-	-	Cavan, Louth, Meath	grouse (warrior)	IG		-	-
(Mac)	Garry (O'Garriga, Garrihy)	IG	-	-	Clare, Leitrim, Roscommon, Ulster	manly	IG		Hare	EN
(Mac)	Gartlan(d)	IG	-	-	Derry, Tyrone	-	-		Garland	NR
(O)	Garvan (Garvey)	IG	-	-	Kerry	rough	IG	Mac	Garvey	IG
Mac	Garvey	IG	-	-	Donegal	rough	IG		-	-
(O)	Garvey	IG	-	-	Armagh, Down	rough	IG		-	-
	Gaskin	FR	FR	13th	Meath	from Gascony	FR		-	-
(O)	Gaughan	IG	-	-	Mayo	anxious	IG		-	-
Mac	Gaughney	IG	-	-	Longford	-	-		Gaffney	IG

Prefix	Surname and Variation	Name Origin*	Migrated From*	Century Estab.	Geographical Locations	Definition of Surname	Language Origin*	Prefix	Pseudonyms and Synonyms	Name Origin*
	Gaule	IG	-	-	Antrim, Kilkenny	foreigner	IG		-	-
(O)	Gavahan (Gaughan)	IG	-	-	Mayo, Roscommon	-	-		-	-
(O)	Gavan (Gavin)	IG	-	-	Cork, Mayo	-	-		-	-
	Gay	EN	EN	-	Clare, Leitrim	-	-		-	-
	Gaynard	NF	EN	13th	Galway, Mayo	-	-		-	-
(Mac)	Gaynor	IG	-	-	Longford	fair head	IG		-	-
(Mac)	Geaney	IG	-	-	Roscommon, Ulster	fettered	IG		-	-
(O)	Geaney	IG	-	-	Cork	fettered	IG		-	-
Mac	Geary (- Gerry)	IG	-	-	Armagh, Tyrone	-	-		-	-
(O)	Geary	IG	-	-	Cork, Roscommon	-	-		-	-
Mac	Gee	SG	SC	-	Derry, Donegal	-	-		-	-
Mac	Gee (Magee)	IG	-	-	Antrim	a form of Hugh	IG		Wynne	WE
(Mac)	Geehan	IG	-	-	Donegal	wind	IG		Wynne	WE
(Mac)	Geoghagen (Gehegan)	IG	-	-	Westmeath	-	-		-	-
	George	SG	SC	17th	Ulster, Waterford	farm worker	SG		Gough	WE
Mac	Geough (- Goff)	IG	-	-	Armagh, Down, Fermanagh, Louth, Monaghan	-	-		Gough	WE
(Mac)	Geraghty (- Geretty)	IG	-	-	Roscommon	member of assembly	IG	(O)	Heraghty	IG

* see definitions

Prefix	Surname and Variation	Name Origin*	Migrated From*	Century Estab.	Geographical Locations	Definition of Surname	Language Origin*	Prefix	Pseudonyms and Synonyms	Name Origin*
Mac	Gettigan (- Ettigan)	IG	-	-	Donegal, Tyrone	-	-		-	-
	Getty (Dalgetty)	SG	SC	-	Antrim, Derry	-	-		-	-
(O)	Giblin	IG	-	-	Roscommon	-	-		-	-
(O)	Gibney	IG	-	-	Cavan, Meath	lock of hair, hound	IG		-	-
	Gibson	SG	SC	-	Antrim, Down	-	-		-	-
(Mac)	Gifford	SG	SC	-	Down	-	-		-	-
	Gilbert	NF	EN	16th	Louth, Meath	-	-		-	-
(Mac)	Gilchrist	IG	-	-	Connacht, Longford	devotee of Christ	IG		-	-
	Gilchrist	SG	SC	-	Ulster	-	-		-	-
(Mac)	Gildea (Kildea)	IG	-	-	Clare, Connacht, Donegal, Leitrim	God	IG		Benison Gay	EN EN
(Mac)	Gilfoyle	IG	-	-	Offaly	devotee of St. Paul	IG		Powell	WE
(Mac)	Gilhooly (Gilhool)	IG	-	-	Leitrim, Limerick, Roscommon, Sligo	shoulder	IG		Cole	EN
Mac	Gill (Magill)	IG	-	-	Ulster	foreigner	IG		Gill	EN
(O)	Gillan (Gillen)	IG	-	-	Donegal, Sligo, Tyrone	lad	IG		-	-
(Mac)	Gillanders	IG	-	-	Monaghan	devotee of St. Andrew	IG		-	-
(Mac)	Gillespie	IG	-	-	Donegal, Down, Galway, Louth	bishop	IG		Bishop Clasby Glashby White	EN EN EN EN
(Mac)	Gilligan (Gillan)	IG	-	-	Derry	lad	IG		-	-

* see definitions

Prefix	Surname and Variation	Name Origin*	Migrated From*	Century Estab.	Geographical Locations	Definition of Surname	Language Origin*	Prefix	Pseudonyms and Synonyms	Name Origin*
	Gillis	SG	SC	-	Ulster	-	-		-	-
	Gillman	FR	EN	16th	Cork	William	FR		-	-
(Mac)	Gilloon	IG	-	-	Derry, Donegal, Fermanagh, Leitrim, Tyrone	-	IG		-	-
Mac	Gillycuddy	IG	-	-	Kerry	devotee of St. Mochuda	IG		-	-
(Mac)	Gilmartin (Kilmartin)	IG	-	-	Connacht, Fermanagh, Tyrone	devotee of St. Martin	IG		Martin	NF
(Mac)	Gilmore	IG	-	-	Ulster	devotee of the Blessed Virgin Mary	IG	Mac	Elmore Elmurray	EN IG
(Mac)	Gilna(g)h	IG	-	-	Longford, Roscommon	of the Saints	IG		Ford	EN
(Mac)	Gilpatrick	IG	-	-	Kilkenny, Laois	son of the devotee of St. Patrick	IG		-	-
(Mac)	Gilpin	EN	EN	-	Armagh, Cavan	-	-		-	-
(Mac)	Gilroy	IG	-	-	Connacht, Ulster	red	IG		-	-
(Mac)	Gils(h)enan	IG	-	-	Fermanagh, Leinster, Tyrone	devotee of St. Senan	IG		Leonard Nugent Gilson	EN NR EN
Mac	Gilvarry	IG	-	-	Connacht, Donegal	devotee of St. Barry	IG		-	-
Mac	Gimpsey	IG	-	-	Down	proud	IG		-	-
Mac	Ginley	IG	-	-	Donegal	fair valor	IG		-	-
(O)	Ginnane (Guinane)	IG	-	-	Clare, Offaly, Tipperary	-	-		-	-
(Mac)	Ginty (Ginity, Maginnity)	IG	-	-	Connacht, Donegal, Monaghan	snow	IG		-	-

* see definitions

Prefix	Surname and Variation	Name Origin*	Migrated From*	Century Estab.	Geographical Locations	Definition of Surname	Language Origin*	Prefix	Pseudonyms and Synonyms	Name Origin*
Mac	Girl (- Gerl, - Garrell)	IG	-	-	Cavan, Donegal, Leitrim	man of valor	IG	Mac	Cargill Gorrell Carkhill	SG IG IG
Mac	Girr (- Geer, - Garr)	IG	-	-	Armagh, Leinster,	short	IG	Mac	Short Gayer	EN EN
(Mac)	Given (Giveen)	IG	-	-	Donegal, Sligo	black, fair	IG		-	-
Mac	Givern	IG	-	-	Armagh, Down	dun-colored	IG		Biggar Guerin Montgomery	SG FR FR
Mac	Givney (- Avinna, - Avinue, - Evinney)	IG	-	-	Cavan	disagreeable	IG		-	-
(Mac)	Glade	SG	SC	-	Ulster	-	-		Lade	EN
(Mac)	Glanny (Glenny)	IG	-	-	Antrim, Derry	of the glen	IG		Hill	EN
	Glanville (Glanfield)	NF	EN	14th	Munster	-	-		-	-
(Mac)	Glashan	IG	-	-	Derry	green or grey - green	IG		Green	EN
(Mac)	Glavin	IG	-	-	Ulster	ruler	IG		Hand	EN
(O)	Glavin	IG	-	-	Cork, Kerry	satirist	IG		-	-
(Mac)	Glavy (Glave)	IG	-	-	Connacht	ruler	IG		Hand	EN
(O)	Gleeson (Glissane)	IG	-	-	Kerry, Tipperary	-	-		-	-
	Glendenning	SG	SC	17th	Antrim, Tyrone	-	-		-	-
(Mac)	Glennon	IG	-	-	Laois, Offaly, Roscommon, Westmeath	cloak	IG		-	-

* see definitions

Prefix	Surname and Variation	Name Origin*	Migrated From*	Century Estab.	Geographical Locations	Definition of Surname	Language Origin*	Prefix	Pseudonyms and Synonyms	Name Origin*
Mac	Glinchy	IG	-	-	Derry, Donegal, Tyrone	mariner	IG		-	-
Mac	Gloin (- Glone, - Gloon)	IG	-	-	Derry, Donegal, Fermanagh, Leitrim Tyrone	devotee of St. John	IG		Monday	EN
(Mac)	Glory (Glowry)	IG	-	-	Armagh, Down, Kilkenny	spokesman	IG		-	-
	Glover	EN	EN	-	Ulster	-	-		-	-
(Mac)	Glynn	IG	-	-	Clare, Roscommon	ruddy	IG		-	-
	Godfrey	EN	EN	-	Fermanagh	-	-		-	-
	Godwin (Goodwin)	EN	EN	-	Clare, Derry, Mayo, Tyrone	good, friend	EN		-	-
	Gogan (Goggin)	IG	-	-	Cork	-	-		-	-
(Mac)	Gogarty	IG	-	-	Meath	-	-		-	-
(O)	Gohery (Geoghery)	NS	-	-	Offaly, Tipperary	-	-		Godfrey	EN
	Going	FR	-	17th	Tipperary	-	-		-	-
	Golden (Goulding)	EN	EN	-	Cork, Leitrim	-	-		-	-
Mac	Gol(d)rick	IG	-	-	Fermanagh, Leitrim	-	-		Golden Goulding	EN EN
Mac	Gonigal (Magonagle)	IG	-	-	Donegal	-	-		Gunnell	EN
	Goodall	EN	EN	16th	Dublin, Wexford	brewer of good ale	EN		-	-
	Goodfellow	EN	EN	-	Tyrone	-	-		-	-

* see definitions

Prefix	Surname and Variation	Name Origin*	Migrated From*	Century Estab.	Geographical Locations	Definition of Surname	Language Origin*	Prefix	Pseudonyms and Synonyms	Name Origin*
	Goodman	EN	EN	17th	Dublin, Monaghan, Tyrone, Wicklow	-	-		-	-
Mac	Goohan	IG	-	-	Leitrim	cuckoo	IG		Caulfield	NE
	Gooley (Goly, Gulley)	IG	-	-	Cork, Limerick	fork	IG		Forke	EN
(O)	Goonan(e)	IG	-	-	Clare	calf keeper	IG		-	-
(O)	Goonery	IG	-	-	Meath	calf keeper	IG		Montgomery	FR
	Gordon	SG	SC	-	Ulster	-	-		-	-
	Gore	EN	EN	17th	Clare, Mayo, Sligo	strip of land	EN		-	-
	Gorham	NF	EN	-	Kerry	-	-		-	-
	Gorham	IG	-	-	Galway	-	-		-	-
(Mac)	Gorman (O' Gorman)	IG	-	-	Clare, Monaghan	-	-		Gorman Grimes Bloomer	IG EN EN
(O)	Gormley (Gormally)	IG	-	-	Donegal, Mayo, Roscommon, Tyrone	-	-		Goff	EN
	Gough	WE	WE	13th	Dublin, Waterford	red	WE		-	-
(O)	Gould (Goold)	EN	EN	-	Cork	gold	EN		Darcy	NF
Mac	Gourkey (- Gourtey)	IG	-	-	Fermanagh, Leitrim	dark	IG		-	-
Mac	Gourneson (Magourahan)	IG	-	-	Ulster	-	-		Somer	EN
Mac	Gover(a)n (- Gowran, Maguran)	IG	-	-	Cavan, Leitrim	summer	IG			

* see definitions

Prefix	Surname and Variation	Name Origin*	Migrated From*	Century Estab.	Geographical Locations	Definition of Surname	Language Origin*	Prefix	Pseudonyms and Synonyms	Name Origin*
	Gow	IG	-	-	Cavan, Meath	blacksmith	IG		Smith	EN
Mac	Gowan	IG	-	-	Cavan	-	-		Smith Gow Going	EN IG FR
	Gowan	IG	-	-	Armagh, Cavan, Down, Leirtrim	-	-		Smith	EN
(O)	Grace	NF	EN	13th	Kilkenny	-	-		-	-
	Grady	IG	-	-	Clare, Limerick, Ulster	illustrious	IG	Mac	Brady Gready	IG IG
(O)	Graham	SG	SC	-	Ulster	-	-	Mac	-	-
	Grainger	FR	-	17th	Leinster, Ulster	farm steward	FR		-	-
Mac	Granahan (- Grenaghan)	IG	-	-	Donegal	sharp-pointed	IG		-	-
(Mac)	Graney (Granny)	IG	-	-	Ulster	pet name for Reginald	IG		Grant	SG
	Granfield (Granville, Grandfield)	NF	EN	16th	Kerry	-	-		-	-
	Grant	SG	SC	16th	Leinstrer, Munster, Ulster	-	-		-	-
	Grath	IG	-	-	Clare, Donegal, Down, Fermanagh, Waterford	-	-		-	-
Mac	Graves (Greaves)	EN	EN	16th	Cork, Offaly, Tyrone	love	IG		Love	EN
	Gray	EN SG	EN SC	-	Connacht, Longford	grove	EN		-	-

* see definitions

Prefix	Surname and Variation	Name Origin*	Migrated From*	Century Estab.	Geographical Locations	Definition of Surname	Language Origin*	Prefix	Pseudonyms and Synonyms	Name Origin*
Mac	Green	IG	-	-	Clare	-	-		Greene	EN
	Greenaway	EN	EN	17th	Galway, Ulster	dweller by the greenway	EN		-	-
	Greenberg	JE	EE	-	Dublin	-	-		-	-
	Green(e)	EN	EN	-	Connacht, Leinster, Munster	-	-		-	-
Mac	Greevy	IG	-	-	Roscommon	grey or brindled	IG		-	-
	Gregory	EN	EN	17th	Galway, Kerry	-	-		-	-
(O)	Grehan (Greaghan)	IG	-	-	Connacht, Westmeath	-	-		Graham, Grimes	SG, EN
(O)	Grennan	IG	-	-	Mayo, Monaghan	sun or sunny	IG		Green	EN
	Grennan (Grennon)	NF	EN	-	Offaly	moustache	NF		-	-
(O)	Griffin (Griffy)	IG	-	-	Clare, Limerick, Tipperary	griffin-like	IG		Griffith, Green	WE, EN
	Griffith	WE	-	-	Kilkenny	-	-		-	-
Mac	Groarke (Grourke)	IG	-	-	Mayo	-	-		-	-
(O)	Groden (Magrudden)	IG	-	-	Connacht	-	-		-	-
Mac	Grod(d)y (- Gruddy)	IG	-	-	Donegal	strong	IG		-	-
(O)	Grogan (Groogan)	IG	-	-	Roscommon, Ulster	hair, fierceness	IG		-	-

* see definitions

Prefix	Surname and Variation	Name Origin*	Migrated From*	Century Estab.	Geographical Locations	Definition of Surname	Language Origin*	Prefix	Pseudonyms and Synonyms	Name Origin*
	Guerin	FR	-	-	Kerry, Limerick, Roscommon, Ulster	-	-	(O)	Geran	IG
								(O)	Gerin	IG
									Green	EN
Mac	Guff (- Giffie)	IG	-	-	Connacht	black	IG		-	-
Mac	Guigan (- Googan)	IG	-	-	Monaghan, Tyrone	-	-		Godwin	EN
									Goodfellow	EN
(O)	Guihan (Guihe(e)n)	IG	-	-	Kerry, Roscommon	wind	IG		-	-
(O)	Guiney (Guinee)	IG	-	-	Cork, Kerry	-	-		-	-
(Mac)	Guinness (- Genis, Magennis)	IG	-	-	Ulster	son of Angus	IG		-	-
Mac	Guire (Maguire)	IG	-	-	Fermanagh	dun-colored	IG		-	-
	Gunn	EN	EN	-	Fermanagh	-	-		-	-
		SG	SC							
	Gunnell	EN	EN	-	Louth	-	-		-	-
(O)	Gunning	IG	-	-	Limerick, Offaly	-	-		-	-
	Gunning	EN	EN	-	Ulster	-	-		-	-
Mac	Gurnahan	IG	-	-	Down	loving, lovable	IG		Gordon	SG
Mac	Gurk (- Guirke)	IG	-	-	Antrim, Down	-	-		-	-
	Guthrie	SG	SC	-	Clare	-	-		-	-
	Guy	FR	-	17th	Ulster	-	-		-	-
	Gwynn (Wynn)	WE	WE	16th	Down, Dublin, Kildare, Longford	white	WE		White	EN

* see definitions

Prefix	Surname and Variation	Name Origin*	Migrated From*	Century Estab.	Geographical Locations	Definition of Surname	Language Origin*	Prefix	Pseudonyms and Synonyms	Name Origin*
	Hackett	NF	EN	12th	Armagh, Connacht, Kildare, Kilkenny, Tyrone	-	-	Mac Mac	Guckian Hackett	IG NF
	Hadden (Haddon)	EN	EN	-	Louth, Ulster	-	-		-	-
	Haddock (Haydock)	EN	EN	17th	Armagh, Kilkenny	-	-		-	-
(O)	Hadian (Hedian)	IG	-	-	Leitrim, Roscommon	-	-		Hadden	EN
(O)	Hagan	IG	-	-	Armagh, Tyrone	young	IG		Aiken Hoge	SG EN
(Mac)	Hague (Haig)	IG	-	-	Cavan	-	-		-	-
(O)	Hahessy	IG	-	-	Galway, Waterford	victorious	IG		-	-
Mac	Hale	IG	-	-	Mayo	companion	IG		Hales Hayles Howell	EN EN WE
	Hale	EN	EN	-	Ulster	-	-		-	-
	Hall	EN	EN	14th	Munster, Ulster	dweller or worker in the hall	EN		-	-
(O)	Hallahan (Hallighan)	IG	-	-	Cork, Waterford	-	-		-	-
(O)	Hall(e)y	IG	-	-	Clare, Tipperary, Waterford	-	-		-	-
(O)	Hallinan	IG	-	-	Limerick, Tipperary, Waterford	noble offspring	IG		Allen Hanlon	EN IG
(O)	Hallion (Hallin)	IG	-	-	Kilkenny, Tipperary	noble rock	IG		Allen	EN

* see definitions

Prefix	Surname and Variation	Name Origin*	Migrated From*	Century Estab.	Geographical Locations	Definition of Surname	Language Origin*	Prefix	Pseudonyms and Synonyms	Name Origin*
(O)	Hallisey	IG	-	-	Cork, Kerry	eagerness	IG		-	-
(O)	Halloran	IG	-	-	Clare, Galway	pirate or stranger	IG		-	-
(O)	Halpenny (Halfpenny, Halpin)	IG	-	-	Limerick, Monaghan	lump	IG		-	-
(O)	Halpin	IG	-	-	Limerick, Monaghan	lump	IG		-	-
(O)	Halvey	IG	-	-	Galway, Leinster, Mayo	noble son	IG		-	-
(O)	Hamill	IG	-	-	Armagh, Monaghan, Tyrone	inactive	IG		Hamilton Hammond	SG EN
	Hamilton	SG	SC	16th	Leitrim, Ulster	-	-		-	-
	Hamlin	NS	-	-	Louth, Meath	-	-		-	-
	Hammond	EN	EN	-	Down	-	-		-	-
	Hampton	EN	EN	14th	Down	-	-		-	-
(O)	Hanafin	IG	-	-	Kerry	storm	-		-	-
(O)	Hanahoe (Hanahy)	IG	-	-	Mayo	-	-		-	-
	Hanbury (Habery)	IG	-	-	Clare, Galway, Mayo	levity, madness	IG		Ansboro	NF
	Hand	EN	EN	-	Dublin, Offaly, Roscommon	-	-		-	-
(O)	Hanley (Handly)	IG	-	-	Cork, Roscommon	beauty	IG		Henley	EN
(O)	Hanlon	IG	-	-	Munster, Ulster	champion	IG		-	-
	Hanna	SG	SC	-	Ulster	-	-		-	-
(O)	Hannavan	IG	-	-	Monaghan	-	-		-	-

* see definitions

Prefix	Surname and Variation	Name Origin*	Migrated From*	Century Estab.	Geographical Locations	Definition of Surname	Language Origin*	Prefix	Pseudonyms and Synonyms	Name Origin*
(O)	Hannigan	IG	-	-	Tyrone, Waterford	-	-		-	-
(O)	Hannon	IG	-	-	Limerick	-	-		-	-
(O)	Hanrahan (Handrahan)	IG	-	-	Clare, Tipperary	-	IG		-	-
(O)	Hanratty (Hanraghty)	IG	-	-	Armagh, Down, Fermanagh, Louth, Monaghan	unlawful	IG		-	-
(O)	Hanvey	IG	-	-	Armagh, Cork, Down, Meath	storm	IG		-	-
O'	Hara (- Hora)	IG	-	-	Antrim, Mayo, Sligo	-	-		-	-
	Hardiman	EN	EN	-	Galway	bold man	EN		Hardy	EN
	Hardman	EN	EN	14th	Meath	hard man, heardsman	EN		-	-
	Hardy	EN	EN	-	Galway	hard	EN		-	-
(O)	Hare	IG	-	-	Armagh	-	-		-	-
	Hare	EN	EN	-	Armagh	-	-		Hardiman	EN
(O)	Hargadan	IG	-	-	Galway	silvery (shinning)	IG		-	-
(O)	Harkin(s) (Harkan)	IG	-	-	Donegal	red	IG		-	-
	Harley	EN	EN	-	Cork	-	-	(O)	Hurley	IG
	Harman (Harmon)	GE	EN	-	Leinster	warrior	GE		-	-
	Harold	NS	-	-	Dublin, Limerick	-	-		Herald	EN
	Harper	EN	EN	16th	Ulster	-	-		-	-

Page 81

* see definitions

Prefix	Surname and Variation	Name Origin*	Migrated From*	Century Estab.	Geographical Locations	Definition of Surname	Language Origin*	Prefix	Pseudonyms and Synonyms	Name Origin*
	Harpur	NF	EN	13th	Leinster	the harper	NF		Harper	EN
(O)	Harran (Herron)	IG	-	-	Donegal	dread	IG		-	-
(O)	Harrigan	IG	-	-	Laois, Munster	-	-		-	-
(O)	Harrihy (Harhoe)	IG	-	-	Donegal, Fermanagh	-	-		Harvey Harris Harrison	EN EN EN
	Harrington	EN	EN	-	Conacht, Cork, Kerry	-	-		-	-
	Harris (Harrison)	EN	EN	16th	Mayo	-	-		-	-
(O)	Harroughton	IG	-	-	Galway, Munster	heroic, tall	IG		Harrington	EN
(O)	Hart	IG	-	-	Meath, Sligo	form of the Christian name Art	IG		-	-
	Hart	EN	EN	16th	Ulster	-	-		-	-
(O)	Hartigan	IG	-	-	Clare, Limerick	form of the Christian name Art	IG		-	-
(O)	Hartily	IG	-	-	Wexford	valor	IG		Hartley	EN
	Harvey	EN	EN	-	Galway, Ulster, Wexford	a measure of grain	EN		-	-
(O)	Hassan	IG	-	-	Derry	deer	IG		-	-
	Hasson	EN	EN	-	Wexford	-	-		-	-
	Hassett	IG	-	-	Clare	-	-		-	-
	Hatch	EN	EN	17th	Louth, Meath	-	-		-	-
(O)	Haugh (Hough)	IG	-	-	Clare, Limerick	-	-		Hawe	EN

* see definitions

Prefix	Surname and Variation	Name Origin*	Migrated From*	Century Estab.	Geographical Locations	Definition of Surname	Language Origin*	Prefix	Pseudonyms and Synonyms	Name Origin*
(O)	Haughan	IG	-	-	Tipperary	-	-		Haughton Hawkins	EN EN
(O)	Haughey (Haffey)	IG	-	-	Armagh, Donegal	-	-		-	-
(O)	Haughihan	IG	-	-	Leinster, Ulster	-	-		Hawkins	EN
	Haughton	EN	EN	-	Tipperary	-	-		-	-
(O)	Haverty	IG	-	-	Galway	-	-		-	-
(O)	Havlin	IG	-	-	Donegal	-	-		-	-
(O)	Hayden	IG	-	-	Carlo, Wexford	-	-		Headon	NF
	Hayes	IG	-	-	Donegal, Mayo, Meath, Monaghan, Tyrone	-	-		-	-
	Hayes	NF	EN	-	Wexford	-	-		-	-
	Hayles (Hales)	EN SG	EN SC	17th	Cork	-	-		-	-
	Hazlett	EN	EN	18th	Ulster	hazel copse	EN		Hayes	NF
(O)	Hea	IG	-	-	Cork	-	-		-	-
	Head(e)	EN	EN	17th	Cork, Galway, Meath, Tipperary, Waterford	source of a stream or valley	EN		-	-
(O)	Healy (Hely)	IG	-	-	Cork, Sligo	ingenious and claimant	IG		Hales Hayles	NE EN
(O)	Heaney (Heeney)	IG	-	-	Armagh, Clare, Derry Fermanagh, Limerick, Mayo	-	-		Bird	EN
	Hearne	EN	EN	-	Waterford	-	-		-	-
	Heatherington	EN	EN	16th	Laois, Tyrone	-	-		-	-

* see definitions

Prefix	Surname and Variation	Name Origin*	Migrated From*	Century Estab.	Geographical Locations	Definition of Surname	Language Origin*	Prefix	Pseudonyms and Synonyms	Name Origin*
(O)	Heaven	IG	-	-	Offaly	swift	IG		Evans	WE
(O)	Heelan	IG	-	-	Munster	-	-		-	-
(O)	Heenan	IG	-	-	Down, Offaly, Tipperary	-	-		-	-
(O)	Heffernan	IG	-	-	Clare, Limerick, Tipperary	-	-		Hernon	IG
(O)	Hegarty	IG	-	-	Munster, Ulster	unjust	IG		-	-
(O)	Hehir (Hegher)	IG	-	-	Clare, Limerick	bitter, sharp	IG		Eyers Hare Ayers	EN EN EN
(O)	Helehan	IG	-	-	Waterford	joyful	IG		-	-
	Hemphill	SG	SC	17th	Derry, Offaly	-	-		-	-
(O)	Henaghan (Henihan)	IG	-	-	Mayo	-	-		Bird	EN
	Hendron	NF	-	-	Armagh	-	-		-	-
	Henderson	EN	EN	-	Ulster	-	-		Henderson	EN
	Henley	EN	EN	-	Mayo	-	-		-	-
(O)	Hennelly	IG	-	-	Mayo	-	-		Henley	EN
(O)	Hennessy	IG	-	-	Cork, Dublin, Meath, Offaly	descendent of Angus	IG		-	-
(O)	Henrick (Han(d)rick)	NS	-	-	Wexford	a form of Henry	NS		-	-
(Mac)	Henry	IG	-	-	Galway, Ulster	easly-roused early	IG		Hendry	EN
(O)	Henry	IG	-	-	Derry, Tyrone	easly-roused early	IG		Harris	EN

* see definitions

Prefix	Surname and Variation	Name Origin*	Migrated From*	Century Estab.	Geographical Locations	Definition of Surname	Language Origin*	Prefix	Pseudonyms and Synonyms	Name Origin*
(O)	Heraghty (Heraty)	IG	-	-	Donegal, Galway, Mayo	member of assembly	IG		Harris	EN
	Herbert	NF	EN	12th	Kerry	-	-		Hobart	EN
(O)	Herlihy	IG	-	-	Cork	underlord	IG	(O)	Hurley	IG
(O)	Hernon	IG	-	-	Galway, Leitrim, Munster	-	-		-	-
(O)	Heskin	IG	-	-	Connacht	-	-		Askin Hoskin Waters	EN EN EN
	Hesselberg	JE	EE	-	Dublin	-	-		-	-
(O)	Hession	IG	-	-	Galway, Mayo	-	-		Ussher	NF
(O)	Hestin (Histon)	IG	-	-	Limerick, Mayo Ulster	-	-		Hastie Hastings	EN EN
	Hewitt	EN	EN	13th	Dublin, Munster, Ulster	diminutive of Hugh	EN		-	-
(O)	Heyne (Hynes)	IG	-	-	Galway	ivy	IG		-	-
(O)	Hickey	IG	-	-	Clare, Limerick, Tipperary	healer	IG		-	-
	Hickman	EN	EN	17th	Clark	hick, pet name for Richard	EN		-	-
(O)	Higgin (Higgins)	IG	-	-	Connacht, Sligo	knowledge, ingenuity	IG		-	-
	Hill	EN	EN	-	Kerry, Ulster	hill	IG		-	-
	Hillery	EN	EN	-	Clare	cheerful	LA		-	-
	Hilliard	GE	EN	17th	Kerry	-	-		-	-

* see definitions

Prefix	Surname and Variation	Name Origin*	Migrated From*	Century Estab.	Geographical Locations	Definition of Surname	Language Origin*	Prefix	Pseudonyms and Synonyms	Name Origin*
	Hilton	EN	EN	17th	Dublin, Ulster	-	-		-	-
(O)	Hiney (Hynie)	IG	-	-	Galway	courage	IG		-	-
(O)	Hingerdell	IG	-	-	Cork, Kerry	-	-		Harrington	EN
(O)	Hingerty	IG	-	-	Cork, Kerry	-	-		Harrington	EN
(O)	Hiskey	IG	-	-	Connacht	-	-		Waters	EN
(O)	Hoban	IG	-	-	Kilkenny, Mayo	-	-		-	-
	Hobart	EN	EN	-	Cork, Kerry	-	-		-	-
	Hobson (Hobbs)	EN	EN	17th	Ulster	diminutive of Robert	EN		-	-
	Hodnett	EN	EN	-	Cork	diminutive of Odo	EN	(Mac)	Sherry	IG
(O)	Hoey	IG EN	- EN	-	Down, Meath, Ulster	-	-		Howe	EN
(O)	Hogan	IG	-	-	Cork, Tipperary	young	IG		-	-
(O)	Hogarty	IG	EN	-	Galway	-	-		Howard	EN
	Hogg	EN	EN	-	Ulster	-	-		-	-
	Holden	EN	EN	-	Kilkenny, Wexford	residence in the hollow valley	EN		Holland	EN
(O)	Holian	IG	-	-	Galway	-	-		-	-
	Holland	EN	EN	-	Clare, Limerick	-	-		-	-
	Hollingsworth	EN	EN	17th	Connacht, Wexford	-	-		-	-
	Holloway	NF	EN	17th	Kildare	-	-	(O)	Halvey	IG
	Hollywood	NF	EN	-	Dublin, Ulster	-	-		-	-

Prefix	Surname and Variation	Name Origin*	Migrated From*	Century Estab.	Geographical Locations	Definition of Surname	Language Origin*	Prefix	Pseudonyms and Synonyms	Name Origin*
	Holmes	SG, EN	SC	16th	All provinces	-	-		-	-
(O)	Holokan (Hoolahan)	IG	-	-	-	-	-		-	-
	Holt	EN	EN	13th	Kilkenny	proud	IG		-	-
(O)	Honan	IG	-	-	Cork, Ulster	a wood	EN		Green	EN
(O)	Honeen	IG	-	-	Clare, Limerick	-	-	(O)	Green, Honan	EN, IG
(O)	Hoolahan	IG	-	-	Clare	green	IG	(O)	Nolan	IG
	Hope	EN	EN	14th	Clare, Connacht, Leinster	proud	IG		-	-
	Hopkins	EN	EN	-	Westmeath	hop a small, enclosed valley	EN		-	-
(O)	Horan	IG	-	-	Connacht, Longford	-	-		-	-
	Hore	NF	EN	-	Cork, Mayo	dun-colored	IG		Howard	EN
(O)	Horgan (Hourigan)	IG	-	-	Wexford	grey-haired or grizzled	NF		-	-
(O)	Horohoe (Hora)	IG	-	-	Cork, Limerick, Tipperary, Waterford	-	-		Harris, Harrison	EN, EN
	Horsey	NF	EN	13th	Mayo	-	-		-	-
(O)	Hounihan (Hoonahan)	IG	-	-	Waterford	-	-		-	-
(O)	Houriskey	IG	-	-	Cork, Limerick	terrible	IG		Caldwell, Waters	EN, EN
	Houston	SG	SC	-	Ulster	vigor	IG		-	-
					Ulster	-	-		-	-

* see definitions

Prefix	Surname and Variation	Name Origin*	Migrated From*	Century Estab.	Geographical Locations	Definition of Surname	Language Origin*	Prefix	Pseudonyms and Synonyms	Name Origin*
	Howard	EN	EN	-	Clare	-	-		-	-
	Howe	EN	EN	-	Meath, Ulster	-	-		-	-
	Howell	WE	-	13th	Mayo	-	-		-	-
Mac	Hugh	IG	-	-	Connacht, Ulster	-	-		Hewson	EN
	Hughes	EN	EN	-	Connacht, Leinster, Ulster	-	-		-	-
Mac	Hugo	IG	-	-	Connacht	-	-		-	-
(O)	Hultaghan	IG	-	-	Fermanagh	Ulsterman	IG	(O)	Nolan	IG
	Hume	EN SG	EN	-	Antrim, Fermanagh	-	-		-	-
	Hunt	EN	EN	-	All provinces	-	-		-	-
(O)	Hurley	IG	-	-	Clare, Cork, Limerick	-	-		Oswell	EN
(O)	Hussey	IG	-	-	Fermanagh, Meath, Tyrone	-	-		-	-
	Hutton	EN	EN	17th	Antrim, Armagh	-	-		-	-
	Hyde	NF	EN	14th	Cork, Kilkenny, Roscommon	-	-		-	-
(O)	Hylan(d)	IG	-	-	Connacht	-	-		Holland Whelan	EN IG
(O)	Hynan (Hinan)	IG	-	-	Limerick, Tipperary	ivy	IG		-	-
Mac	Ildoon	IG	-	-	Armagh	chief of the fort	IG		-	-
Mac	Ildowney (- Eldowney)	IG	-	-	Down	son of the devotee of the church	IG		-	-
Mac	Ilduff (Duff)	IG	-	-	Cavan, Tyrone	black	IG		-	-

* see definitions

Prefix	Surname and Variation	Name Origin*	Migrated From*	Century Estab.	Geographical Locations	Definition of Surname	Language Origin*	Prefix	Pseudonyms and Synonyms	Name Origin*
Mac	Ilhatton (- Clatton, - Hatton)	IG	-	-	Antrim, Derry	devotee of St. Catan	IG		-	-
Mac	Ilhoyle (- Coyle)	IG	-	-	Donegal, Monaghan	devotee of St. Comga	IG		Woods	EN
Mac	Ilmurray (- Elmurry)	IG	-	-	Derry, Fermanagh, Tyrone	devotee of the blessed Virgin Mary	IG	(Mac)	Gilmore	IG
Mac	Ilpatrick (Gilpatrick)	IG	-	-	Kilkenny, Laois	devotee of St. Patrick	IG		-	-
Mac	Ilroy (- Gilroy, - Elroy)	IG	-	-	Connacht, Ulster	red	IG		Roy	FR
Mac	Ilveen (- Elveen, Kilveen)	IG	-	-	Down	gentle	IG		-	-
Mac	Ilwaine (- Elwain)	IG	-	-	Sligo	white	IG	(Mac)	Kilbane	IG
Mac	Ilwaine	SG	SC	-	Ulster	-	-		-	-
Mac	Inerney (- Inerkney, Kinnerk)	IG	-	-	Clare	church steward	IG		-	-
	Ingoldsby	EN	EN	-	Antrim, Donegal, Monaghan	-	-		-	-
	Ingram	SG	SC	17th	Limerick, Ulster	-	-		Ennis	IG
Mac	Innes	SG	SC	-	Uslter	-	-		-	-
Mac	Intyre	SG	SC	-	Ulster	craftsman	SG		-	-
	Ireland	EN	EN	-	Antrim, Armagh	-	-		-	-
	Irvine (Ervine)	SG	SC	17th	Ulster	-	-		Irwin Erwin	EN EN
	Irwin (Erwin)	EN	EN	-	Roscommon, Ulster	boar friend	EN		-	-

* see definitions

Prefix	Surname and Variation	Name Origin*	Migrated From*	Century Estab.	Geographical Locations	Definition of Surname	Language Origin*	Prefix	Pseudonyms and Synonyms	Name Origin*
	Ivers (Ivis)	EN	EN	-	Clare	-	-		-	-
Mac	Ivor (- Iver)	NS	NS	-	Tyrone	-	-		-	-
	Ivory	FR	EN	17th	Waterford	-	-		-	-
	Jack	EN / FR	EN / -	- / -	Antrim, Donegal, Down, Kilkenny, Tyrone	pet name for John / pet name for Jacques	FR / EN		-	-
	Jackman	EN	EN	-	Waterford	-	-		-	-
	Jackson	EN	EN	17th	Ulster	-	-		-	-
	Jacob	EN	EN	14th	Laois, Wexford	-	-		-	-
	Jago (Macego, Mackigo)	EN	-	16th	Cork, Longford, Roscommon	derivative of Jacob	CO		-	-
	James	EN	EN	-	Ulster	-	-		-	-
Mac	James	IG	-	-	Carlow, Wicklow	-	-		-	-
	Jameson	SG	SC	18th	Ulster	-	-		-	-
	Jennings	NS	-	-	Armagh, Down, Fermanagh, Galway, Louth, Mayo, Monaghan	diminutive of Jan or Jen	NS		-	-
	Jephson	EN	EN	17th	Cork	-	-		-	-
	Jermyn	GE	GE	13th	Munster	The German	GE		-	-
	Jervois (Jervis)	FR	-	14th	Cork	-	-		-	-
	Johnson	SG	SC	-	Ulster	-	-	Mac	Johnson	-
	Johnston(e)	EN	EN	-	Ulster	-	-		-	SG

Prefix	Surname and Variation	Name Origin*	Migrated From*	Century Estab.	Geographical Locations	Definition of Surname	Language Origin*	Prefix	Pseudonyms and Synonyms	Name Origin*
	Jolley (Joly)	FR	-	16th	Clare, Dublin Limerick, Waterford	festive	FR		-	-
	Jones	WE	-	-	All Provinces	-	-		-	-
	Jordan	IG	-	-	All Provinces	-	-	Mac	Stephens	IG
	Joy	FR	-	-	Connacht, Kerry, Waterford	-	-		-	-
	Joyce	WE	-	-	Galway, Mayo	-	-		Joy	FR
	Joynt	FR	-	-	Limerick, Mayo	slim, graceful	-		-	-
	Judge	EN	EN	-	Sligo	-	-		-	-
	Julian	NF	EN	-	Meath	-	-		-	-
(O)	Kanavaghn	IG	-	-	Sligo	-	-		Conway	IG
(O)	Kane (O' Cahan)	IG	-	-	Derry, Tyrone	-	-		Cain Cane	EN EN
	Kavanagh	IG	-	-	Wexford	-	-		Cavandish	EN
Mac	Kay	SG	SC	-	Ulster	-	-		-	-
(Mac)	Keady	IG	-	-	Cork, Galway, Laois	hundred	IG		-	-
(O)	Kealaghan (Kel(e)laghan)	IG	-	-	Armagh	companion	IG		-	-
(O)	Keal(l)y (Keeley)	IG	-	-	Laois, Louth, Meath	-	-		Wisdom	EN
Mac	Kean	SG	SC	-	Derry, Donegal	a variant of Eoin (John)	SG		-	-
(Mac)	Keane (Mac Cahan)	IG	-	-	Clare	-	-		-	-

* see definitions

Prefix	Surname and Variation	Name Origin*	Migrated From*	Century Estab.	Geographical Locations	Definition of Surname	Language Origin*	Prefix	Pseudonyms and Synonyms	Name Origin*
(O)	Keane	IG	-	-	Waterford	-	-		-	-
(O)	Keaney	IG	-	-	Donegal, Galway, Leitrim	-	-		-	-
Mac	Kearney	IG	-	-	Ulster	victorious	IG		-	-
(O)	Kearney (Carney)	IG	-	-	Mayo, Meath, Tipperary	victorious, warlike	IG		Fox	EN
(O)	Keary (Keery)	IG	-	-	Leinster	black or dark brown	IG		Carey	EN
	Keating	NF	EN	-	Leinster, Tipperary	-	-		-	-
(O)	Keaty	IG	-	-	Limerick	sense	IG		Keating	NF
(O)	Keaveney (Geaveney)	IG	-	-	Connacht	-	-		Keyes Kavanagh	EN IG
(Mac)	Kee	IG	-	-	Ulster	son of Hugh	IG		Eason	EN
(O)	Keefe	IG	-	-	Cork	gentle	IG		-	-
(O)	Keegan	IG	-	-	Dublin, Leitrim, Roscommon, Wicklow	-	-		-	-
(Mac)	Keehan	IG	-	-	Clare	blind	IG		-	-
(O)	Keelan (Keelahan)	IG	-	-	Armagh, Down, Fermanagh, Louth, Meath, Monaghan	-	-		-	-
	Keeling	EN	EN	17th	Dublin	-	-		-	-
(O)	Keenan (Kinahan)	IG	-	-	Fermanagh, Offaly, Roscommon	fair offspring	IG		-	-
(Mac)	Keeney (Keagney, Keangy)	IG	-	-	Fermanagh, Tyrone	-	-		-	-
(O)	Keeshan (Kissane)	IG	-	-	Clare, Tipperary	-	-		-	-

* see definitions

Prefix	Surname and Variation	Name Origin*	Migrated From*	Century Estab.	Geographical Locations	Definition of Surname	Language Origin*	Prefix	Pseudonyms and Synonyms	Name Origin*
(O)	Keevan (Kevane)	IG	-	-	Cork, Mayo, Sligo	having long locks of hair	IG		-	-
Mac	Keever (- Keevers)	IG	-	-	Monaghan, Tyrone	-	-	Mac	Ivor	NS
(O)	Kegley	IG	-	-	Carlow, Donegal, Mayo, Monaghan, Wexford, Waterford	-	-		-	-
(Mac)	Kehilly	IG	-	-	Cork	blind, hero	IG		Coakley	EN
(O)	Keighron	IG	-	-	Galway	hungry person	IG		-	-
(Mac)	Keighry	IG	-	-	Galway	-	-		Carey	EN
	Keirsey (Kiersey)	NF	EN	13th	Waterford	-	-		-	-
(O)	Kelleher	IG	-	-	Cork, Kerry	companion dear	IG		Keller	GE
	Kells (Kell)	NS	-	-	Antrim, Cavan, Monaghan	cauldron	NS		-	-
(O)	Kelly	IG	-	-	Derry, Galway, Laois, Meath, Roscommon, Wicklow	strife	IG		-	-
Mac	Kelvy (- Elwee)	IG	-	-	Donegal	lad, yellow	IG	Mac	Calvey	IG
	Kemp	EN	EN	14th	Antrim, Down, Dublin	athlete	IG		-	-
(Mac)	Kendrick (Kenrick, Condrick)	GE	-	-	Munster, Ulster	home rule	GE		-	-
	Kenefick	WE	-	13th	Cork	-	-		-	-
Mac	Kenna (Kennagh)	IG	-	-	Clare, Kerry, Monaghan	-	-		-	-
(Mac)	Kennan (Kinnane)	IG	-	-	Armagh, Louth, Monaghan	-	-		-	-

* see definitions

Prefix	Surname and Variation	Name Origin*	Migrated From*	Century Estab.	Geographical Locations	Definition of Surname	Language Origin*	Prefix	Pseudonyms and Synonyms	Name Origin*
(O)	Kennedy	IG	-	-	Clare, Tipperary, Wexford	head, ugly	IG		Minnagh	IG
(O)	Kennelly	IG	-	-	Munster	-	-		-	-
(O)	Kenny	IG	-	-	Donegal, Galway	-	-		-	-
	Kent	EN	EN	13th	Meath	-	-		-	-
Mac	Kenzie	SG	SC	-	Ulster	-	-		Kinney	IG
	Keogan	IG	-	-	Cavan, Meath	-	-		-	-
(Mac)	Keogh (Kehoe)	IG	-	-	Limerick, Roscommn, Tipperary, Wexford, Wicklow	-	-		-	-
(Mac)	Keo(g)hane (Kohane)	IG	-	-	Cork	-	-	(Mac)	-	-
Mac	Keon (- Keown)	IG	-	-	Armagh, Down, Fermanagh, Galway, Monaghan	both names are forms of John	IG		Caulfield Johnson Johnston Owen Bissett	EN SG EN WE SG
(Mac)	Keoneen	IG	-	-	Galway, Mayo	little John	IG		-	-
(Mac)	Kermode (- Dermot)	IG	-	-	Connacht	-	-		-	-
(O)	Kernaghan	IG	-	-	Antrim, Armagh, Donegal	victorious	IG		-	-
	Kerr	SG	SC	-	Ulster	-	-		-	-
(O)	Kerrane	IG	-	-	Donegal, Mayo	-	-		Carey	EN
(O)	Kerrigan	IG	-	-	Galway, Mayo, Sligo	black or dark brown	IG		Comber	EN
(O)	Kerry	IG	-	-	Kildare, Meath, Westmeath	-	-		-	-

* see definitions

Prefix	Surname and Variation	Name Origin*	Migrated From*	Century Estab.	Geographical Locations	Definition of Surname	Language Origin*	Prefix	Pseudonyms and Synonyms	Name Origin*
Mac	Kervey	IG	-	-	Fermanagh	gambler	IG		-	-
(O)	Kett	IG	-	-	Clare	-	-		-	-
	Kettle	NS	-	-	Dublin, Louth	-	-		-	-
Mac	Kettrick	SG	SC	-	Sligo	-	-		-	-
(O)	Kevane	IG	-	-	Kerry, Mayo, Sligo	long locks of hair	IG		Cavendish	EN
Mac	Kibbin (- Gibbon)	IG	-	-	Antrim, Down	a diminutive form of Philip	IG		-	-
	Kidd	EN	EN	-	Ulster	-	-		-	-
	Kidney	EN	EN	-	Cork	-	-		-	-
(O)	Kielty	IG	-	-	Munster, Ulster	slender	IG		Woods Small	EN EN
(O)	Kieran (Kerin)	IG	-	-	Connacht, Cork, Fermanagh, Monaghan	black or dark brown	IG		Cairns Carey Kerr	SG EN SG
(Mac)	Kiernan (Keran, - Kernan)	IG	-	-	Cavan, Fermanagh Leitrim	lord	IG		Lord	EN
(Mac)	Kiggins (Kiggin)	IG	-	-	Connacht	a diminutive form of Hugo	IG		-	-
(Mac)	Kilbane	IG	-	-	Sligo	white	IG		White	EN
(Mac)	Kilbride (- Bride, Gilbride)	IG	-	-	Connacht	devotee of St. Brigid	IG		-	-
(Mac)	Kilcash	IG	-	-	Sligo	devotee of St. Cas.	IG		-	-
(Mac)	Kilcline	IG	-	-	Roscommon	deceitful	IG		Clynes	IG
(Mac)	Kilcommon(s)	IG	-	-	Galway, Roscommon	devotee of St. Coman	IG		-	-
(Mac)	Kilcooly (Cooley)	IG	-	-	Clare, Galway	servant of St. Mochuille	IG		-	-

* see definitions

Prefix	Surname and Variation	Name Origin*	Migrated From*	Century Estab.	Geographical Locations	Definition of Surname	Language Origin*	Prefix	Pseudonyms and Synonyms	Name Origin*
(Mac)	Kilcoyne (Coyne)	IG	-	-	Connacht	gentle	IG		-	-
Mac	Kilcullen	IG	-	-	Mayo, Sligo	devotee of St. Cailin	IG		-	-
(Mac)	Kilderry (Kildare)	IG	-	-	Clare	-			-	-
(Mac)	Kilduff (- Elduff, Gilduff, Duff)	IG	-	-	Galway	black	IG		-	-
(Mac)	Kildunn (Dunn)	IG	-	-	Sligo	brown	IG		-	-
(Mac)	Kilgallen (Kilcullen)	IG	-	-	Mayo, Sligo	devotee of St. Cailin	IG		-	-
(Mac)	Kilgannon	IG	-	-	Sligo	-			-	-
(Mac)	Kilgore	IG	-	-	Ulster	-			-	-
(Mac)	Kilgrew (Kilgrove)	IG	-	-	Waterford	-			Killigrew	EN
(Mac)	Kilkelly (Killykelly)	IG	-	-	Galway	devotee of St. Ceallach	IG		-	-
(Mac)	Kilkenny (- Elhinney, - Ilhenny)	IG	-	-	Connacht, Ulster	devotee of St. Canice	IG		-	-
(O)	Killeen	IG	-	-	Clare, Galway, Mayo, Offaly	-			-	-
(O)	Killian (Killion, Killeen)	IG	-	-	Clare, Galway, Roscommon, Westmeath	-			-	-
(Mac)	Killoran (Gilloran)	IG	-	-	Roscommon	-			-	-
(Mac)	Kilpatrick	IG	-	-	Ulster	-			Kirkpatrick	SG

* see definitions

Prefix	Surname and Variation	Name Origin*	Migrated From*	Century Estab.	Geographical Locations	Definition of Surname	Language Origin*	Prefix	Pseudonyms and Synonyms	Name Origin*
(Mac)	Kilroy (Kilroe)	IG	-	-	Roscommon	red	IG		-	-
(Mac)	Kimm	SG	SC	-	Derry	-	-		-	-
(O)	Kinahan	IG	-	-	Roscommon, Ulster	-	-		-	-
	Kincaid (Kinkead)	SG	SC	17th	Antrim, Derry	-	-		-	-
	Kincart	IG	-	-	Dublin, Ulster	right	IG		Wright	EN
(O)	Kindelan	IG	-	-	Meath, Westmeath	gracefully shaped	IG		-	-
	King	EN	EN	-	Connacht, Ulster	-	-		-	-
	Kingsley	EN	EN	-	Carlow, Wexford	-	-		-	-
	Kingston	EN	EN	17th	Cork, Dublin, Sligo	-	-		-	-
Mac	Kinley	SG	SC	-	Antrim	fair hero	SG		-	-
Mac	Kinn (- Ginn)	IG	-	-	Derry, Mayo	fair	IG		King	EN
(O)	Kinnane (Quinane)	IG	-	-	Tipperary	-	-	O	Guinane	IG
Mac	Kinnawe (Kinneavy)	IG	-	-	Kerry, Leitrim	hound, swim	IG		Ford	EN
(O)	Kinneally	IG	-	-	Limerick	head wolf	IG		-	-
	Kinnear	SG	SC	-	Ulster	-	-		-	-
(Mac)	Kinneen	IG	-	-	Connacht	rabbitt	IG		Rabbitt	EN
(Mac)	Kinney	IG	SC	-	Fermanagh, Tyrone	-	-		-	-
Mac	Kinney	SG	SC	-	Antrim, Tyrone	-	-		-	-
	Kinsella	IG	-	-	Carlow, Wexford	-	-		Kingsley	EN

* see definitions

Prefix	Surname and Variation	Name Origin*	Migrated From*	Century Estab.	Geographical Locations	Definition of Surname	Language Origin*	Prefix	Pseudonyms and Synonyms	Name Origin*
Mac	Kinstry (- Nestry)	SG	SC	-	Ulster	traveler	SG		-	-
(O)	Kirby (Kervick, Kerwick, Kerribly)	IG	-	-	Kilkenny, Limerick, Mayo, Waterford	black or dark brown	IG		-	-
	Kirk(e)	EN	EN	-	Ulster	-	-		-	-
	Kirkpatrick	SG	SC	-	Ulster	-	IG	(Mac)	Kilpatrick	IG
(O)	Kirwin	IG	-	-	Galway	black	IG		-	-
(O)	Kissane	IG	-	-	Cork, Kerry	tribute or rent	IG		Cashman	EN
Mac	Kitterick (-Ketrick, - Kitterick)	NS	-	-	Armagh, Down, Fermanagh, Louth, Monaghan	-	-		Hanson	IG
	Knapp	EN	EN	17th	Cork	hillock	EN		-	-
	Knaresborough	EN	EN	-	Kilkenny	-	-		-	-
(O)	Kneafsey	IG	-	-	Donegal	bone	IG		Bonar	GE
	Knightly	EN	EN	17th	Kerry	-	-		-	-
	Knipe	EN	EN	17th	Armagh, Cavan	ridge	EN		-	-
	Knott (Canute)	EN	EN	17th	Dublin	thickset person	EN		-	-
	Knowland	EN	EN	-	Longford, Westmeath	-	-		-	-
	Kyle	SG	SG	16th	Derry	-	-		-	-
(O)	Kyne	IG	-	-	Connacht	wild goose	IG		Barnacle Coyne	EN FR
(O)	Lacken	IG	-	-	Connacht	-	-		Duck	EN
(de)	Lacy	NF	EN	12th	Limerick, Meath	-	-		-	-

* see definitions

Prefix	Surname and Variation	Name Origin*	Migrated From*	Century Estab.	Geographical Locations	Definition of Surname	Language Origin*	Prefix	Pseudonyms and Synonyms	Name Origin*
	Lacy	IG	-	-	Wexford	prince	IG		-	-
	Lade (Laide)	EN	EN	17th	Kildare, Tipperary	dweller by the forest	EN		-	-
	Laffan	NF	EN	14th	Tipperary, Wexford		-		-	-
(O)	Laffey	IG	-	-	Clare, Galway, Kildare		-		-	-
(O)	Laherty	IG	-	-	Kilkenny, Tipperary		-		-	-
(O)	Lahiff (Lahire)	IG	-	-	Clare, Galway, Kerry	ruler	IG		Guthrie Lahy	SG IG
	Lahy	IG	-	-	Clare, Kilkenny		-		-	-
Mac	Lain (-Clean)	SG	SC	-	Antrim, Derry	a form of Eoin (John)	SG		-	-
	Laird	SG	SC	-	Ulster	Lord	SG		-	-
	Laly	IG	-	-	Roscommon		-		-	-
(O)	Lalor (Lawler)	IG	-	-	Laois	half, sick person	IG		-	-
	Lambert (Lamport)	SG	SC	17th	Galway, Leinster, Mayo		-		-	-
	Lamont (Lammon)	SG	SC	-	Ulster		-		-	-
	Landers (Landra, Landry, Londra, London)	NF	EN	12th	Dublin, Meath, Wexford	London	NF		Glanders	IG
(de)	Landon	NF	EN	13th	Limerick, Waterford		-		-	-
	Landy	NF	EN	13th	Kilkenny, Tipperary	glade	NF		-	-
	Lane	EN	EN	-	Cork, Limerick		-		-	-

* see definitions

Prefix	Surname and Variation	Name Origin*	Migrated From*	Century Estab.	Geographical Locations	Definition of Surname	Language Origin*	Prefix	Pseudonyms and Synonyms	Name Origin*
	Lang	SG	SC	-	Ulster	-	-		-	-
(O)	Langan	IG	-	-	Armagh, Mayo	tall	IG		-	-
	Langford	EN	EN	16th	Kerry, Limerick, Ulster	-	-		-	-
	Langshire	EN	EN	17th	Kilkenny	-	-		-	-
	Langton	EN	EN	-	Kilkenny	-	-		-	-
(O)	Lanigan	IG	-	-	Kilkenny	-	-		-	-
(O)	Lappin	IG	-	-	Armagh, Derry, Donegal Fermanagh, Tyrone	-	-		Delap	EN
	Lardner	EN	EN	-	Galway	-	-		-	-
Mac	Lardy	SG	SC	-	Antrim, Down	-	-		-	-
	Large	NF	-	13th	Antrim, Galway	generous	NF		-	-
(O)	Larkin (Lorkin)	IG	-	-	Galway, Monaghan, Tipperary, Wexford	rough or fierce	IG		-	-
	Larmour (Larmer, Armour)	FR	-	17th	Ulster	the armourer	FR		-	-
(O)	Larrissy	IG	-	-	Kilkenny, Mayo	sea, vigor	IG		-	-
(O)	Lasty (Lusty)	IG	-	-	Donegal	-	-		-	-
	Latimer	SG	SC	17th	Cavan, Monaghan	-	-		-	-
	Latouche	FR	FR	17th	Dublin	-	-		-	-
	Lattin	EN	EN	14th	Kildare	-	-		-	-
	Lauder (Lawder)	IG	-	-	Leinster	strong	IG		-	-

Page 100

* see definitions

Prefix	Surname and Variation	Name Origin*	Migrated From*	Century Estab.	Geographical Locations	Definition of Surname	Language Origin*	Prefix	Pseudonyms and Synonyms	Name Origin*
(O)	Laughane	IG	-	-	Cork, Mayo, Meath	grey	IG		Lawton	EN
Mac	Lauren	SG	SC	-	Ulster	son of Lawrence	SG		Lawson	EN
	Lavelle	IG	-	-	Connacht, Donegal	movement	IG		Falls Melville	NF
(O)	Laverty (Lafferty)	IG	-	-	Donegal, Tyrone	-	-		-	-
(O)	Lavery (Lowry)	IG	-	-	Antrim, Down	spokesman	IG		Armstrong	EN
(O)	Lavin	IG	-	-	Roscommon	ruler	IG		Hand	EN
	Law(e)	EN	EN	-	Ulster	-	-		-	-
	Lawless	EN	EN	-	Dublin, Galway, Kilkenny	-	-		-	-
(O)	Lawn (Lehane)	IG	-	-	Cork, Donegal, Sligo	-	-		-	-
	Lawrence (Laurence)	EN	EN	17th	Donegal, Dublin, Tipperary, Tyrone	-	-		-	-
	Lawson	EN	EN	17th	Ulster	-	-		-	-
	Lawton	EN	EN	-	Cork	-	-		-	-
	Leach (Leech)	EN	-	-	Galway	doctor	EN		-	-
(O)	Leahy	IG	-	-	Cork, Kerry, Tiperary	heroic	IG		Lahy	IG
(O)	Lean (Lyne)	IG	-	-	Cork, Kerry	-	-		Lyons	EN
(O)	Leany	IG	-	-	Munster	descendent of the Leinsterman	IG		-	-
(O)	Leary	IG	-	-	Cork	-	-		-	-

* see definitions

Prefix	Surname and Variation	Name Origin*	Migrated From*	Century Estab.	Geographical Locations	Definition of Surname	Language Origin*	Prefix	Pseudonyms and Synonyms	Name Origin*
(Mac)	Leavy (Levy)	IG	-	-	Longford	hound, mountain	IG		-	-
	Lecky (Lackey, Leakey)	SG	SC	17th	Carlow, Derry, Donegal	-	-		-	-
	Ledger (Legear)	GE	-	-	Limerick	people, spear	GE		-	-
	Lee	EN	EN	-	Laois	-	-		-	-
(Mac)	Lee	IG	-	-	Connacht	-	-		-	-
(O)	Lee	IG	-	-	Cork, Limerick	-	-		Leigh	EN
	Leeper	EN	EN	17th	Donegal	runner or jumper	EN		-	-
	Legge	EN	EN	-	Ulster	-	-		-	-
(O)	Lehane (Leehan)	IG	-	-	Cork, Limerick	grey	IG		Lane Lyons	EN EN
	Leigh	EN	EN	-	Connacht, Cork, Limerick	-	-		-	-
Mac	Lellan (- Clelland, - Leland)	SG	SC	-	Sligo	-	-		-	-
	Lemass	FR	-	18th	Carlo, Dublin	-	-		-	-
	Lemon	EN	EN	-	Ulster	-	-		-	-
	Lendrum	SG	SC	17th	Fermanagh, Tyrone	-	-		-	-
(O)	Lenihan (Lenaghan, Linehan)	IG	-	-	Cork, Limerick, Roscommon	-	-		-	-
Mac	Lennon (- Lennan)	SG	SC	17th	Galway	-	-		Leonard	EN
(O)	Lennon (Lennan)	IG	-	-	Cork, Fermanagh, Galway	cloak or mantle	IG		Leonard	EN

* see definitions

Prefix	Surname and Variation	Name Origin*	Migrated From*	Century Estab.	Geographical Locations	Definition of Surname	Language Origin*	Prefix	Pseudonyms and Synonyms	Name Origin*
	Leo	EN	EN	-	Limerick	water	LA		-	-
	Leonard	EN	EN	-	All Provinces	-	-		-	-
	Leslie	SG	SC	17th	Monaghan	-	-		-	-
	Lestrange	IG	-	-	Offaly, Westmeath	border hound	IG		-	-
	Lestrange	EN	EN	16th	Westmeath	-	-		-	-
	Lett	EN	EN	17th	Wexford	joy	EN		-	-
	Levi (Levy)	JE	EE	-	Dublin	-	-		-	-
	Lewis	EN SG WE	- - -	-	All Provinces	-	-		-	-
(O)	Liddy (Leddy)	IG	-	-	Cavan, Clare, Limerick, Tipperary	-	-		-	-
	Lightfoot (Lighterfoot)	EN	EN	17th	Ulster	-	-		-	-
	Lilly	IG	-	-	Fermanagh	-	-		-	-
(Mac)	Limerick	FR	-	-	Derry	-	-		-	-
	Lindsay	SG	SC	-	Ulster	-	-		-	-
(O)	Linnane	IG	-	-	Munster	-	-		Leonard	EN
(O)	Linnegar (Linneen)	IG	-	-	Fermanagh	-	-		Leonard	EN
	Lipsett	GE	-	-	Donegal	-	-		-	-
	Liston	NF	EN	13th	Limerick	-	-		-	-
	Little	EN	EN	-	Dublin, Mayo, Meath	-	-		Littleton	EN

* see definitions

Page 103

Prefix	Surname and Variation	Name Origin*	Migrated From*	Century Estab.	Geographical Locations	Definition of Surname	Language Origin*	Prefix	Pseudonyms and Synonyms	Name Origin*
	Litton	EN	EN	15th	Dublin, Meath	-	-		-	-
(O)	Loan(e)	IG	-	-	Monaghan	hound, warrior	IG		Lambe	EN
	Locke	EN	EN	16th	Cork, Dublin	lock of hair	EN		-	-
	Loftus	EN	EN	16th	Mayo	-	-		-	-
	Logan (Lohan, Lagan)	NF SG IG	- - -	- - -	Antrim, Down	-	-		-	-
	Logue (Loogue)	IG	-	-	Clare, Connacht, Derry, Donegal, Leinster	-	-	(O)	Molloy	IG
(O)	Lohan (Loghan, Loughan, Logan)	IG	-	-	Galway, Westmeath	-	-		Chaff Duck	EN EN
	Lomasney (Lemasney)	IG	-	-	Tipperary	bare, rib	IG		-	-
	Lombard	FR	FR	13th	Cork	banker	FR		-	-
(O)	Lonergan (Londrigan)	IG	-	-	Tipperary	-	-		-	-
	Long (Longan)	IG EN NF	- EN EN	- - -	Cork, Donegal	-	-		-	-
	Longan	IG	-	-	Limerick	tall	IG		Long	EN
	Longfield	EN	EN	17th	Cork	-	-		-	-
(O)	Loonane	IG	-	-	Longford	hound, warrior	IG		-	-
(O)	Looney (Loonan)	IG	-	-	Clare	hound, warrior	IG		Clooney	IG
	Lord	EN	EN	17th	Dublin, Westmeath	-	-		-	-

* see definitions

Prefix	Surname and Variation	Name Origin*	Migrated From*	Century Estab.	Geographical Locations	Definition of Surname	Language Origin*	Prefix	Pseudonyms and Synonyms	Name Origin*
(O)	Losty (Lasty, Lastly, Lusty)	IG	-	-	Donegal		-		Leslie	SG
Mac	Loughlin (- Laughlin)	NS	-	12th	Derry, Donegal		-			-
(O)	Loughlin	IG	-	-	Clare, Limerick, Tipperary		-	(O)	Loughnane	IG
	Loughman (Loughnan)	IG	-	-	Kilkenny, Laois		-			-
(O)	Loughnane (Loughnan)	IG	-	-	Cork, Mayo, Meath	grey	IG		Lawton Loftus	EN EN
(O)	Loughran	IG	-	-	Armagh, Tyrone	bright	IG		Lochran	IG
(O)	Loughrey	IG	-	-	Ulster		-			-
	Love	EN	EN	17th	Derry		-			-
	Lovell	FR	EN	14th	Kilkenny	wolf cub	FR			-
	Lowe	EN	EN	-	Dublin, Ulster		-			-
	Lowney	IG	-	-	Cork		-			-
	Lowry	SG	SC	-	Ulster		-			-
	Lowther	EN	EN	16th	Fermanagh		-			-
(Mac)	Loy	IG	-	-	Ulster		-		Lowe	EN
(O)	Luby (Looby)	IG	-	-	Tipperary	cunning	IG			-
	Lucas	EN	EN	14th	Leinster, Munster, Ulster		-			-
	Lucy	EN	EN	-	Fermanagh		-			-

* see definitions

Page 105

Prefix	Surname and Variation	Name Origin*	Migrated From*	Century Estab.	Geographical Locations	Definition of Surname	Language Origin*	Prefix	Pseudonyms and Synonyms	Name Origin*
	Lucey	IG	-	-	Cork	-	-		-	-
(O)	Ludlow	EN	EN	14th	Cork, Dublin, Louth Meath, Ulster	-	-		-	-
	Lundy	NF	EN	-	Derry, Kilkenny, Tipperary	-	-		-	-
	Lunney	IG	-	-	Tyrone	-	-		Leonard	EN
(O)	Lusk	IG	-	-	Dublin, Ulster	-	-		-	-
	Luttrell	FR	-	13th	Dublin	the otter	FR		-	-
(O)	Lydon (Leyden, Liddane)	IG	-	-	Calre, Galway, Mayo	-	-		-	-
	Lyle (Lisle)	FR	SC	-	Antrim, Derry, Down	-	-		-	-
(O)	Lynagh (Leynagh)	IG	-	17th	Galway, Kildare, Mayo, Meath	the Leinsterman	IG		-	-
	Lynan (Lynam)	IG	-	-	Carlow	-	-		Lynham	EN
	Lynch (deLench)	NF	EN	-	Antrim, Cavan, Clare, Cork, Galway, Tipperary	-	-		Lindsey	SG
	Lynch (Linchy, Lynchehan)	IG	-	-	All Provinces	mariner	IG		-	-
(O)	Lynchehan	IG	-	-	Donegal, Tyrone	-	-		-	-
(O)	Lyne (Lean)	IG	-	-	Cork, Kerry	-	-		Lyons Lane	EN EN
	Lyness	EN	EN	17th	Antrim, Armagh, Down	-	-		-	-
(O)	Lynn	IG	-	-	Antrim	-	-		Lindsey	SG

* see definitions

Prefix	Surname and Variation	Name Origin*	Migrated From*	Century Estab.	Geographical Locations	Definition of Surname	Language Origin*	Prefix	Pseudonyms and Synonyms	Name Origin*
	Lyon	SG	SC	-	Ulster	-	-		-	-
	Lyons	EN	EN	-	Cork, Galway	-	-		Lane	EN
(Mac)	Lysaght (Lysaught)	IG	-	-	Clare, Dublin, Limerick	loaned	IG		-	-
	Lyvet	NF	EN	13th	Leinster	-	-		-	-
Mac	Ma (-Magh)	IG	-	-	Ulster	son of Matthew	IG		-	-
(Mac)	Macken (Mackin)	IG	-	-	Louth, Monaghan	son, youth	IG		-	-
	Macken	IG	-	-	Cork, Mayo	son, youth	IG		-	-
	Mackey	IG	-	-	Tipperary	-	IG		-	-
	Mackle (O' Mackell)	IG	-	-	Armagh	-	-		-	-
(O)	Madden	IG	-	-	Galway, Kildare	-	-		-	-
	Madden	EN	EN	-	Kildare	-	-		-	-
	Maddock (Maddox)	WE	-	-	Down, Wexford	-	-		Mayduck	EN
(O)	Madigan	IG	-	-	Clare, Limerick	-	-		-	-
(O)	Ma(g)han (Maughan)	IG	-	-	Galway	-	-		-	-
	Maghery	IG	-	-	Armagh, Limerick	of the field	IG		Field	EN
	Magourahan	IG	-	-	Down	-	-		Gordon	SG
	Mahaffy (Macafee, Machaffy, Macfie)	SG	SC	-	Donegal	peace-making, black-haired man of peace	SG		-	-

* see definitions

Prefix	Surname and Variation	Name Origin*	Migrated From*	Century Estab.	Geographical Locations	Definition of Surname	Language Origin*	Prefix	Pseudonyms and Synonyms	Name Origin*
(O)	Maher (Meagher)	IG	-	-	Offaly, Tipperary	hospitable	IG		-	-
Mac	Mahon	IG	-	-	Clare, Monaghan	bear	IG		Mann Matthews	EN EN
(O)	Mahony	IG	-	-	Cork	bear	IG		-	-
(O)	Mahood (Machood, O' Hood)	IG	-	-	Antrim	-	-		Hood	EN
(O)	Mailie	IG	-	-	Connacht	-	-		-	-
	Maisel	JE	EE	Dublin	-	-	-	-	-	-
	Major	EN	EN	17th	Ulster	-	-		-	-
	Malick	IG	-	-	Offaly, Roscommon, Westmeath	-	-		-	-
(O)	Maliffe	IG	-	-	Galway	black chief	IG		-	-
O'	Malley (Mailey, Malia)	IG	-	-	Mayo	-	-		-	-
(O)	Mallon (Mallin)	IG	-	-	Armagh, Tyrone	peasant	IG		-	-
(O)	Malone (Maloon, Muldoon)	IG	-	-	Clare, Offaly	devotee of St. John	IG		-	-
(O)	Maloney (Malony)	IG	-	-	Clare, Tipperary	servant of the church	IG		-	-
(O)	Manahan (Manihan)	IG	-	-	Cork	monk	IG		-	-
de	Mandeville (Mansfield)	NF	EN	13th	Antrim, Tipperary, Waterford	-	-	Mac Mac Mac	Cullen Cullen William Quillan	IG IG SG IG

* see definitions

Prefix	Surname and Variation	Name Origin*	Migrated From*	Century Estab.	Geographical Locations	Definition of Surname	Language Origin*	Prefix	Pseudonyms and Synonyms	Name Origin*
(O)	Mangan (Mongan, Mingane)	IG	-	-	Connacht, Limerick, Tyrone	hairy	IG		-	-
	Manley (Mannelly, Manly)	IG EN	- EN	-	Cork				-	-
	Mann (Magnus)	SG	SC	-	Ulster				-	-
	Mann	EN	EN	-	Meath				-	-
(O)	Mannin (Mannion)	IG	-	-	Galway				Manning Matthews	EN EN
	Manning	EN	EN	-	Cork, Dublin	monk	IG		-	-
	Mannix	IG	-	-	Cork				-	-
Mac	Manus	NS	-	-	Fermanagh, Roscommn	from the Norse name of Manus	NS		Mayne	EN
(O)	Markahan (Markey)	IG	-	-	Clare				Markham Ryder	EN EN
(O)	Markey	IG	-	-	Louth, Monaghan	rider	IG		Markham Marks Ryder	EN EN EN
	Mark(s) (Markes)	EN	EN	17th	Laois, Ulster				-	-
(O)	Marron (Merren)	IG	-	-	Armagh, Monaghan, Sligo	quick, lively	IG		-	-
	Marsh	EN	EN	17th	Leinster, Ulster	marsh or fen	EN		-	-
	Marshall	NF	EN	-	Ulster				-	-
	Martin (Martyn)	EN IG SG	EN - SC	-	Galway, Tyrone, Westmeath				-	-
	Mason	EN	EN	13th	Leinster, Munster, Ulster				-	-

* see definitions

Prefix	Surname and Variation	Name Origin*	Migrated From*	Century Estab.	Geographical Locations	Definition of Surname	Language Origin*	Prefix	Pseudonyms and Synonyms	Name Origin*
	Massey	EN	EN	-	Limerick	-	-		-	-
Mac	Master	SG	SC	-	Antrim, Down, Longford	son of the master	SG		-	-
Mac	Master	IG	-	-	Cavan, Leitrim	-	-		-	-
	Masterson	EN	EN	16th	Wexford	-	-		-	-
Mac	Math (- Meath, - Maugh)	SG	SC	17th	Ulster	-	-		-	-
	Mather(s)	EN	EN	17th	Armagh, Down, Dublin	mower	EN		Matthews	EN
	Matthews	EN	EN	-	Louth, Ulster	-	-		-	-
	Matufsky	JE	EE	-	Dublin	-	-		-	-
	Maude	EN	EN	17th	Galway, Kilkenny	-	-		-	-
	Maxwell	SG	SC	-	Ulster	-	-		-	-
	Maybury (Mayberry)	EN	EN	-	Kerry, Ulster	-	-		-	-
	Mayne	EN	EN	-	Antrim, Fermanagh	-	-		-	-
(Mac)	Mayo (Mayhew, Mahew)	IG	-	-	Mayo	not derived from the name of the county	-		-	-
	Meade	IG EN	- EN	- -	Cork, Meath	-	-		-	-
(O)	Meagher (Maher)	IG	-	-	Offaly, Tipperary	kindly	IG		-	-
(O)	Meany	IG	-	-	Clare, Kilkenny	-	-		-	-
O'	Meara (- Mara)	IG	-	-	Tipperary	merry	IG		-	-

* see definitions

Prefix	Surname and Variation	Name Origin*	Migrated From*	Century Estab.	Geographical Locations	Definition of Surname	Language Origin*	Prefix	Pseudonyms and Synonyms	Name Origin*
	Meares (Mayers, Mair, Mairs)	EN	EN	-	Dublin, Ulster	-	-		-	-
(O)	Mee (Mea)	IG	-	-	Down, Mayo, Roscommon, Westmeath	honorable	IG		May	EN
(O)	Meehan	IG	-	-	All Provinces	honorable	IG		-	-
(O)	Meenagh (Minnagh)	IG	-	-	Ulster	thorns	IG		-	-
(O)	Meenaghan (Minnagh, Minaghan)	IG	-	-	Mayo, Roscommon	Munsterman	IG		-	-
(O)	Meenan	IG	-	-	Donegal	goodwill	IG		-	-
(O)	Meere	IG	-	-	Clare	mirth	IG		Myers	EN
(O)	Mehegan (Meehan)	IG	-	-	Cork, Sligo	soft	IG		-	-
(O)	Melaghlin	IG	-	-	Westmeath	devotee of St. Seachlann	IG	Mac	Loughliin	NS
	Mellan (Mellon)	IG	-	-	Armagh, Tyrone	pleasant	IG		Monroe Munroe	SG SG
(O)	Mellerick	IG	-	-	Cork, Connacht	devotee of St. Cyriacus	IG		-	-
(O)	Melly	IG	-	-	Connacht, Donegal	pleasant	IG		-	-
(O)	Melody	IG	-	-	Clare, Galway, Offaly, Westmeath	head, ugly	IG		-	-
	Melville (Mulvihill)	NF	-	-	Ulster	-	-		-	-

* see definitions

Prefix	Surname and Variation	Name Origin*	Migrated From*	Century Estab.	Geographical Locations	Definition of Surname	Language Origin*	Prefix	Pseudonyms and Synonyms	Name Origin*
Mac	Menamin (- Manamon, - Manamy, - Menamy, - Mananay)	IG	-	-	Donegal, Mayo, Roscommon, Tyrone	high spirits	IG		-	-
	Menarry (Mac Nary, Mac Neary)	IG	-	-	Armagh, Down, Fermanagh, Louth	modest	IG		-	-
	Mercer (Mercier)	FR	-	16th	Antrim, Down, Offaly	merchant	FR		-	-
	Meredith	WE	-	16th	Leinster, Munster, Ulster	magnificent	WE		-	-
	Mernagh	IG	-	-	Wexford	deft	IG		-	-
(O)	Merrigan (Maragin)	IG	-	-	Longford, Westmeath	-	-		Morgan	WE
	Merry	IG	-	-	Tipperary, Waterford	lively	IG	(O)	Holohan	IG
(O)	Mescal	IG	-	-	Calre, Galway, Limerick, Waterford	-	-		Maxwell	SG
	Meyer (Meyers, Meere)	IG EN FR GE	EN - -	- - -	All Provinces	-	-		-	-
(Mac)	Meyler	WE	-	13th	Wexford	-	-		-	-
	Michael	EN	EN	-	Connacht	-	-		Mitchell	EN
Mac	Millan	SG	SC	-	Ulster	-	-		-	-
	Millar (- Miller)	EN	EN	-	Antrim	-	-		-	-
(O)	Millea	IG	-	-	Connacht, Kilkenny	devotee of St. Hugh	IG	(O)	Miley Melay Mealue	IG IG IG

* see definitions

Prefix	Surname and Variation	Name Origin*	Migrated From*	Century Estab.	Geographical Locations	Definition of Surname	Language Origin*	Prefix	Pseudonyms and Synonyms	Name Origin*
	Millett (Mellot, Mylotte)	IG	-	-	Galway, Kilkenny, Mayo, Tipperary	soldier	IG		-	-
(O)	Milligan (Milliken)	IG	-	-	Antrim, Derry	-	-		-	-
	Mills	EN	EN	-	Ulster	of the mill	EN		-	-
	Milne	EN	EN	18th	Dublin	workers at the mill	EN		-	-
(O)	Milroy (Mulry)	IG	-	-	Longford, Mayo	red chief	IG		Monroe	SG
	Minnagh	IG	-	-	Tyrone	Munsterman	IG		-	-
	Minnis (Mac Neece, Mannice, Mac Nish)	SG	SC	-	Uslter	-	-		-	-
(O)	Minogue (Minnock)	IG	-	-	Clare, Tipperary	monk	IG		Mannix Monaghan	IG IG
	Miskelly	IG	-	-	Antrim	-	-		-	-
	Mitchell (Mulvihill)	EN	EN	-	Connacht, Leinster, Ulster	-	-		-	-
	Moffat (Maffett, Mefatt)	SG	SC	17th	Ulster	-	-		-	-
(O)	Mohan (Mahon, Moan)	IG	-	-	Galway, Monaghan, Sligo	-	IG		Vaughan	WE
(O)	Moher	IG	-	-	Clare, Cork, Waterford	overgrown with brushwood	-		-	-
de	Moleyns	NF	EN	-	Clare, Cork, Kerry	-	-		-	-
(O)	Molloy (Mulloy)	IG	-	-	Derry, Donegal, Kerry, Monaghan, Offaly, Roscommon	big and soft, noble	IG		Molyneux	FNK

* see definitions

Prefix	Surname and Variation	Name Origin*	Migrated From*	Century Estab.	Geographical Locations	Definition of Surname	Language Origin*	Prefix	Pseudonyms and Synonyms	Name Origin*
(O)	Molon(e)y	IG	-	-	Clare, Cork, Tipperary	servant of the church	IG		-	-
	Molyneux	NF	EN	-	Kerry	-	-		-	-
(O)	Monaghan	IG	-	-	Armagh, Down, Fermanagh, Louth, Roscommon	monk	IG		Monks	EN
Mac	Monagle (- Monigal)	IG	-	-	Donegal	wealthy, valor	IG		-	-
(O)	Mongney (Mungay)	IG	-	-	Meath	-	-		Montgomery	FR
	Monks	EN	EN	-	Connacht	-	-		-	-
(O)	Monnelly (Monley)	IG	-	-	Mayo	wealthy, valor	IG		Manley	EN
	Monroe (Munroe)	SG	SC	-	Ulster	-	-		-	-
	Montagu(e)	NF	EN	-	Armagh, Tyrone	-	-		-	-
	Montgomery	FR	-	17th	Cork, Louth, Ulster	-	-	Mac	Goonery, Mongney, Givern	IG, IG, IG
	Moody (Mody)	EN	EN	13th	Offaly, Ulster	brave or impetous	EN		-	-
(O)	Mooney (Meaney, Meeney, Mainey)	IG	-	-	Donegal, Munster, Offaly, Sligo	dumb	IG		-	-
	Moore	EN	EN	-	Antrim, Dublin	-	-		-	-
	Moorehead (Muirhead)	SG	SC	-	Ulster	-	-		-	-
(O)	Mora	IG	-	-	Kerry, Laois	-	-		-	-

* see definitions

Prefix	Surname and Variation	Name Origin*	Migrated From*	Century Estab.	Geographical Locations	Definition of Surname	Language Origin*	Prefix	Pseudonyms and Synonyms	Name Origin*
(O)	Morahan (Moran)	IG	-	-	Galway, Leitrim, Mayo, Offaly	sea warrior	IG		Morrin Morgan Markan	FR SG IG
(O)	Moran (Morahan)	IG	-	-	Fermanagh, Galway, Leitrim, Mayo, Offaly	-	-		Morrin	FR
(O)	Morchoe	IG	-	-	Wexford	sea warrior	IG		-	-
O'	More	IG	-	-	Laois	majestic	IG		Moore	EN
	Morgan	WE	-	-	Antrim, Armagh, Down, Dublin, Fermanagh, Louth, Monaghan	-	-		-	-
(O)	Moriarty	IG	-	-	Kerry	navigator	IG		-	-
(O)	Moroney	IG	-	-	Clare, Kerry	-	-		-	-
(O)	Morrally (Morley)	IG	-	-	Mayo	valor	IG		Morley	EN
	Morrin	FR	-	-	Offaly	-	-		-	-
	Morris	NF	EN	-	Galway	-	-		-	-
Mac	Morris (- Morrish)	IG	-	-	Kerry, Mayo	-	-		Fitzmaurice	NF
	Morrison	EN	EN	-	Ulster	-	-		Bryson	EN
	Morrissey	IG NF	- EN	-	Kilkenny, Sligo, Tipperary, Waterford	sea, action	IG		Morris	NF
	Morrow	EN	EN	-	Ulster	-	-		-	-
Mac	Morrow	IG	-	-	Fermanagh, Leitrim	mariner	IG		-	-
	Mortimer	FR	EN	14th	Connacht, Meath	-	-		-	-
	Morton	EN	EN	13th	Dublin, Ulster	-	-		-	-

* see definitions

Prefix	Surname and Variation	Name Origin*	Migrated From*	Century Estab.	Geographical Locations	Definition of Surname	Language Origin*	Prefix	Pseudonyms and Synonyms	Name Origin*
	Moss (Malmona, Mulmona)	EN	EN	-	Donegal, Fermanagh	moorland or turf bog	EN		-	-
	Motley (Motlowe, Mutlone)	EN	EN	14th	Leinster	-	-		-	-
(O)	Moy	IG	-	-	Donegal	-	-		-	-
	Moy	EN	EN	17th	Ulster	-	-		-	-
(O)	Moylan	IG	-	-	Clare, Cork, Tipperary	-	-		-	-
	Moyle (Moyles)	IG	-	-	Mayo	bald	IG		Miles	EN
	Moynihan (Minihan, Munster)	IG	-	-	Cork, Kerry, Mayo	Munsterman	IG		-	-
(O)	Muckley (Mulclahy)	IG	-	-	Munster, Sligo	game, stone	IG	(O)	Mulcahy Stone	IG EN
	Mularkey	IG	-	-	Galway, Mayo, Sligo	-	-		-	-
(O)	Mulcahy (Cahy, Caughery, Mac Cahy)	IG	-	-	Down, Tipperary	derived from St. Cathach	IG		-	-
(O)	Mulcreevy (Mulgrievy)	IG	-	-	Armagh, Down	-	-		Rice	IG
(O)	Mulderrig	IG	-	-	Mayo	red chief	IG		Reddington Reid Rutledge	EN EN EN
(O)	Muldoon (Malone)	IG	-	-	Clare, Galway, Ulster	fort	IG		-	-
(O)	Muldowney	IG	-	-	Ulster	servant of the church	IG	Mac Mac	Downey Downey Gildowney Gildowney	IG IG IG

* see definitions

Prefix	Surname and Variation	Name Origin*	Migrated From*	Century Estab.	Geographical Locations	Definition of Surname	Language Origin*	Prefix	Pseudonyms and Synonyms	Name Origin*
(O)	Mulgeehy	IG	-	-	Donegal	wind	IG		Wyndham Wynne	EN WE
(O)	Mulgrew (Grew)	IG	-	-	Armagh, Tyrone	-	-		-	-
(O)	Muhall	IG	-	-	Laois	devotee of St. Cathal	IG	(O)	Halley	IG
(O)	Mulholland	IG	-	-	Derry, Donegal, Limerick, Meath, Westmeath	devotee of St. Calann	IG		Holland	EN
(O)	Mulkerrin (Mulkerrill)	IG	-	-	Galway, Roscommon	devotee of St. Kieran	IG		-	-
Mac	Mullen (- Mullan)	IG	-	-	Antrim, Down	bald	IG	Mac	Millan	SG
(O)	Mullery (Mulry)	IG	-	-	Mayo, Roscommon	devotee of the Blessed Virgin Mary	IG		Miles	EN
(O)	Mulligan	IG	-	-	Donegal, Mayo, Monaghan	bald	IG		Baldwin Molyneux	GE NF
(O)	Mullin (Mullen, Mullins, Mellon, Mac Mullen)	IG	-	-	Connacht, Ulster	bald	IG	Mac de	Millan Moleyns	SG NF
(O)	Mullock (Mulock)	IG	-	-	Galway, Leitrim, Roscommon	derived from the personnal name Milo	IG	(O)	Molloy	IG
(O)	Mulloon (Malone)	IG	-	-	Clare	devotee of St. John	IG		-	-
(O)	Mullover	IG	-	-	Mayo	harvest	IG		Milford Palmer	EN NF
(O)	Mulqueeny (Mulqueen, Mulligan, Mulkeen)	IG	-	-	Clare, Mayo	servant of St. Caoine	IG		-	-
(O)	Mulready	IG	-	-	Roscommon	devotee of St. Brigid	IG		Reid	EN

* see definitions

Prefix	Surname and Variation	Name Origin*	Migrated From*	Century Estab.	Geographical Locations	Definition of Surname	Language Origin*	Prefix	Pseudonyms and Synonyms	Name Origin*
(O)	Mulreavy	IG	-	-	Donegal	brindled or swathy	IG		-	-
(O)	Mulrennan	IG	-	-	Roscommon	devotee of St. Brennan	IG		-	-
(O)	Mulrooney (Moroney, Rooney)	IG	-	-	Galway, Fermanagh	-	-		-	-
(O)	Mulroy (Mulry, Milroy, Mullgry)	IG	-	-	Longford, Mayo	red chief	IG		Munroe	SG
(O)	Mulvanaughty (Mulvanerty, Mulvanerton)	IG	-	-	Leitrim	blessing	IG		Blessing	EN
(O)	Mulvan(n)y (Mulvenna)	IG	-	-	Leinster, Ulster	-	IG		-	-
(O)	Mulvey (Mulveagh)	IG	-	-	Clare, Leitrim	honorable	IG		-	-
(O)	Mulvihill (Mulville, Melville)	IG	-	-	Clare, Galway, Roscommon, Ulster	devotee of St. Michael	IG		Melville Mitchell Michael	NF EN EN
(O)	Mulvogue	IG	-	-	Connacht, Donegal	devotee of St. Mogue	IG	(O)	Molloy	IG
(O)	Murdoch	SG	SC	-	Ulster	-	-		-	-
(O)	Murnane (Marrinane, Marnane)	IG	-	-	Clare, Cork, Limerick, Tipperary	-	-		Warren	FR
(Mac)	Murphy (Morphy)	IG	-	-	Antrim, Cork, Kerry, Tyrone	sea warrior	IG		-	-
(O)	Murphy (Morphy)	IG	-	-	Cork, Kerry, Roscommon, Wexford	sea warrior	GA		-	-
(O)	Murray (Murry)	SG	SC	-	Donegal	-	-		-	-

* see definitions

Prefix	Surname and Variation	Name Origin*	Migrated From*	Century Estab.	Geographical Locations	Definition of Surname	Language Origin*	Prefix	Pseudonyms and Synonyms	Name Origin*
Mac	Murray	IG	-	-	Down	-	-		-	-
Mac	Murrough	IG	-	-	Wexford	-	-		Morrow, Redmond	EN, NF
(O)	Murry (MacElmurray, Gilmore)	IG	-	-	Galway, Roscommon	-	-		Morrow	EN
(O)	Murrihy	IG	-	-	Clare	-	-		-	-
Mac	Murtagh	IG	-	-	Leinster	navigator	IG		Murray	SG
Mac	Murtagh (Murdoch)	SG	SC	-	Ulster	-	-		-	-
	Myers	EN	EN	-	Clare	-	-		-	-
Mac	Nabb	SG	SC	-	Ulster	abbot	SG		-	-
Mac	Naboe	IG	-	-	Cavan, Longford	premature	IG		Victory	EN
Mac	Naboola	IG	-	-	Sligo	the hound of Boyle	IG		Benbo	EN
(O)	Naghten (Nocton, Knochton, Nation)	IG	-	-	Clare, Galway, Roscommon	bright or pure	IG	Mac	Norton, Knight, Naughton	EN, EN, SG
	Nagle (Nangle)	NF	EN	-	Connacht, Leinster	-	-		-	-
Mac	Nair	SG	SC	-	Ulster	-	-		-	-
(Mac)	Nally (- Anally)	IG	-	-	Armagh, Cork, Derry, Down, Fermanagh, Louth, Mayo, Roscommon	poor man	IG		-	-
Mac	Nalty (- Naulty, - Analty)	IG	-	-	Connacht, Ulster	wild, hound	IG		-	-
Mac	Namara	IG	-	-	Clare	hound of the sea	IG		-	-

* see definitions

Prefix	Surname and Variation	Name Origin*	Migrated From*	Century Estab.	Geographical Locations	Definition of Surname	Language Origin*	Prefix	Pseudonyms and Synonyms	Name Origin*
Mac	Namee	IG	-	-	Tyrone	hound of the meath	IG	-	-	-
(Mac)	Nanny	IG	-	-	Roscommon	hound of the fair	IG	-	Leonard	EN
-	Napper (Napier)	FR	EN	17th	Meath	maker of table cloths	-	-	-	-
Mac	Naughton	SG	SC	-	Ulster	-	-	(O) Mac	Naghten Cracken	IG SG
(Mac)	Naulty (- Analty, Nolty)	IG	-	-	Connacht, Uslter	hound, wild	IG	-	-	-
-	Naylor	EN	EN	17th	Dublin, Limerick, Offaly	-	-	-	-	-
(Mac)	Neale	SG	SC	-	Ulster	-	-	-	-	-
-	Neale	EN	EN	-	Ulster	-	-	-	-	-
(O)	Neary	IG	-	-	Connacht	modest	IG	-	-	-
Mac	Nee (- Neagh, - Nay)	SG	SC	-	Connacht	champion	SG	-	-	-
(O)	Nee (Needham)	IG	-	-	Galway, Limerick, Mayo	champion	IG	-	-	-
(Mac)	Neely	IG	-	-	Galway	hound	IG	-	-	-
(O)	Neenan (Noonan)	IG	-	-	Clare	child	IG	-	-	-
(O)	Neeson	IG	-	-	Monaghan, Tyrone	-	-	-	-	-
(O)	Neilan	IG	-	-	Clare	-	-	-	-	-
Mac	Neil	SG	SC	14th	Antrim, Derry, Mayo	-	-	-	-	-
(O)	Neill	IG	-	-	Antrim, Down, Carlow, Tipperary, Tyrone, Waterford	the Norse	IG	-	-	-

* see definitions

Prefix	Surname and Variation	Name Origin*	Migrated From*	Century Estab.	Geographical Locations	Definition of Surname	Language Origin*	Prefix	Pseudonyms and Synonyms	Name Origin*
	Neilson (Nelson)	NS		17th	Dublin, Ulster					
Mac	Neish (-Nish)	SG	SC		Ulster					
	Neligan	IG	SC		Cork, Kerry					
(O)	Nelis (-Nellis)	IG			Donegal	vigor	IG			
Mac	Nesbitt	EN			Cavan					
	Neville	FR	EN		Clare, Limerick, Kilkenny, Wexford					
	Nevin (Knavin, Navin)	IG	EN		All provinces	bone	IG		Bowen	WE
(Mac)	Newcombe (Newcomen)	EN		16th	Dublin, Mayo					
	Newell	IG	EN	13th	Kildare	envy, valor	IG		Knowles	EN
	Newell	EN	EN		Down				Knowles	EN
(O)	Newman	EN	EN		Cork, Dublin, Meath					
	Newsom	EN	EN		Cork					
	Neylan (Neilan)	IG			Caire, Connacht	the Norse	IG			
(O)	Nicholas	NF	EN		Tyrone, Waterford				Clausson	NF
Mac	Nix	IG			Limerick				Woulfe	NF
(Mac)	Nixon	EN	EN	17th	Fermanagh, Wicklow					
	Noble	NF	EN	13th	Ulster	wellknown, noble	NF			
	Noel	FR			Antrim, Down, Dublin	Christmas	FR			

* see definitions

Prefix	Surname and Variation	Name Origin*	Migrated From*	Century Estab.	Geographical Locations	Definition of Surname	Language Origin*	Prefix	Pseudonyms and Synonyms	Name Origin*
(O)	Nolan (Knowland)	IG	-	-	Carlow, Fermanagh, Longford, Mayo, Roscommon	shout	IG	(O)	Holohan	IG
								(O)	Hultaghan	IG
(O)	Noonan (Nunan)	IG	-	-	Cork	beloved	IG		-	-
	Norman	NF	EN	-	Derry, Dublin	man from the North	NF		-	-
	Norris	FR	EN	-	Leinster, Munster, Ulster	northerner /Norseman	FR		Nurse	NF
									Nourse	NF
									Northridge	EN
	Nugent	NF	EN	-	Cork, Westmeath	-	-		-	-
	Nulty	IG	-	-	Donegal, Louth, Meath	Ulsterman	IG		-	-
	Nunn	EN	EN	17th	Wexford	-	-		-	-
(O)	Nyhan (Nihane)	IG	-	-	Cork	-	-		-	-
	Oakes	EN	EN	-	Antrim	-	-		-	-
	Oates	EN	EN	-	Tipperary	-	-		-	-
	Odell	NS	-	17th	Louth, Ulster	-	-		-	-
	Odlum (Adlam)	GE	EN	17th	Offaly	-	-		-	-
	Oliver	NF	EN	14th	Limerick, Louth, Ulster	-	-		-	-
	Orchard	EN	EN	-	Tipperary, Ulster, Wexford	-	-		-	-
	Ormond	IG	-	-	Cork, Waterford	-	IG		Augher	IG
	Ormsby	EN	EN	16th	Connacht	red	-		Roe	EN
	Orr	SG	SC	17th	Ulster	-	-		-	-

Prefix	Surname and Variation	Name Origin*	Migrated From*	Century Estab.	Geographical Locations	Definition of Surname	Language Origin*	Prefix	Pseudonyms and Synonyms	Name Origin*
	Osborne	EN	EN	16th	Louth, Meath, Sligo, Tipperary, Waterford	-	-		-	-
Mac	Oscar	GE	-	-	Ulster	-	-		-	-
Mac	Ostrich	SG	SC	-	Cork	-	-		-	-
	Oswell (Oswald)	EN	EN	-	Ulster	-	-		-	-
	Ovens	EN	EN	-	Fermanagh	furnace	EN		-	-
	Owens	WE	-	-	Ulster	-	-		-	-
	Padden (Padine)	IG	-	-	Connacht	diminutive of Patrick	IG		Patterson Pattison	EN EN
	Page	EN	EN	16th	Galway, Ulster	-	-		-	-
	Paisley	SG	SC	17th	Ulster	-	-		-	-
	Pakenham	EN	EN	16th	Westmeath	-	-		-	-
	Palmer	NF	EN	13th	Mayo	the palmer, pilgrim	NF		-	-
	Parker	FR	-	17th	Ulster	park keeper	FR		-	-
	Parkinson	EN	EN	17th	Ulster	-	-		-	-
	Parle (Parill)	NF	EN	16th	Clare, Wexford	diminutive of Peter	NF		-	-
	Parnell	EN	EN	17th	Dublin, Longford, Wicklow	derivative of Peter	EN		-	-
Mac	Parlon (Parlone)	IG	-	-	Armagh, Leitrim, Tyrone	-	-		Parnell	EN
	Parsons	EN	EN	16th	Offaly	-	-		-	-
	Partlan (Parlan)	IG	-	-	Ulster	-	-		Bartley	EN

* see definitions

Page 123

Prefix	Surname and Variation	Name Origin*	Migrated From*	Century Estab.	Geographical Locations	Definition of Surname	Language Origin*	Prefix	Pseudonyms and Synonyms	Name Origin*
	Partridge	EN	EN	-	Dublin, Ulster	a bird	EN		Patrick Partrick	SG SG
Mac	Patrick	SG	SC	-	Longford, Ulster	-	-	Mac	-	-
	Patterson (Pattison)	EN	EN	-	Galway, Ulster	-	-		-	-
	Payne	EN	EN	14th	Dublin, Tipperary	-	-		-	-
	Peacock	EN	EN	15th	All provinces	-	-		-	-
	Peake	IG	-	-	Derry, Tryone	thickest man	EN		Pike	-
	Peake	EN	EN	-	Leinster	-	-		-	-
	Pearson	NF	EN	17th	Leinster	son of Piers	NF		-	-
	Peebles	SG	SC	-	Ulster	-	-		-	-
	Pelly	EN FR	EN EN	17th	Galway, Roscommon	-	-		-	-
	Pembroke	WE	-	17th	Kerry, Kilkenny	-	-		-	-
	Pennefather	EN	EN	17th	Linster, Munster	penny father	EN		-	-
	Penny	EN	EN	13th	Cork, Dublin	-	-		-	-
	Penrose	EN	EN	17th	Waterford, Wicklow	-	-		-	-
	Peoples	EN	EN	-	Donegal	-	-	(O)	Deeney Peebles	IG SG
	Peppard	FR	-	17th	Louth, Meath, Wexford	-	-		Pepper Piper	NF EN
	Perdue	FR	-	-	Cork	-	-		-	-
	Perrot	IG	-	-	Cork	derivative of Peter	IG		-	-
	Perry	EN	EN	17th	Munster, Ulster	pear, tree	NF		-	-

* see definitions

Prefix	Surname and Variation	Name Origin*	Migrated From*	Century Estab.	Geographical Locations	Definition of Surname	Language Origin*	Prefix	Pseudonyms and Synonyms	Name Origin*
	Petane	IG	-	-	Donegal, Galway, Mayo	deminutive of Patrick	IG		-	-
	Pettigrew (Petticrew)	FR	SC	17th	Ulster	small growth	FR		-	-
	Petty (Petit, Pettitt)	NR	EN	17th	Kerry, Meath, Westmeath	little	NF		Little	EN
	Peyton (Payton, Patton)	EN	EN	12th	Donegal	diminutive of Patrick	EN		-	-
(O)	Phelan	IG	-	-	Kilkenny, Waterford	wolf	IG		-	-
(Mac)	Philbin	NF	EN	-	Galway, Mayo	diminutive of Philip	NF		Phillips Plover	EN EN
	Phillips	EN	EN	-	Galway, Mayo				-	-
Mac	Phillips	SG	SC	-	Cavan, Monaghan				-	-
	Phylan (Fyland, Philan)	IG	-	-	Offaly, Ulster, Westmeath			(Mac)	Philbin	NF
	Pickens	SG	SC	17th	Cavan				-	-
	Pierce (Pearse)	EN IG	EN	-	Kerry, Leinster				-	-
	Pigot (Piggott)	FR	-	16th	All provinces				Beckett	FR
	Pim	EN	EN	17th	Dublin, Laois				-	-
	Piper	EN	EN	-	Ulster				-	-
	Plant	EN	EN	17th	Longford, Wicklow				-	-
	Plummer (Plumer)	EN	EN	17th	Cork, Limerick	plumber, plumer (dealer in feathers)	EN		-	-
	Plunket[t]	FR	FR	12th	Meath				-	-
	Poe	EN	EN	17th	Kilkenny, Tipperary, Tyrone				-	-

Prefix	Surname and Variation	Name Origin*	Migrated From*	Century Estab.	Geographical Locations	Definition of Surname	Language Origin*	Prefix	Pseudonyms and Synonyms	Name Origin*
(Mac)	Polin (Poland)	IG	-	-	Armagh, Down, Offaly	diminutive of Paul	IG		-	-
	Pollard	EN	EN	14th	Westmeath	close-cropped head, derivative of Paul	EN		-	-
	Pope	EN	EN	16th	Dublin, Waterford	-	-		-	-
	Porteous	SG	SC	16th	Kilkenny, Laois, Ulster	-	-		-	-
	Porter	EN	EN	13th	Leinster, Munster, Ulster	-	-		-	-
	Powell	WE	-	-	All provinces	-	-		-	-
	Power	NF	NR	12th	Waterford	poor man	NF		-	-
	Pratt (Pendy, Pindy)	EN	EN	-	Cork	-	-		-	-
	Prendergast	NF	NR	12th	Mayo, Tipperary	-	-	Mac	Fitzmaurice Morris Pindy	NF IG NF
	Prenderville (Pendy, Pindy)	NF	EN	13th	Kerry	-	-		Pindy Pendy	NF NF
	Prescott	EN	EN	15th	Antrim, Down, Dublin Kilkenny, Meath	priest's cottage	EN		-	-
	Preston	NF	EN	13th	Meath	-	-		-	-
(O)	Prey (Pray)	IG	-	-	Armagh, Down	-	-		-	-
	Price	WE	-	14th	Ulster	-	-		-	-
	Pringle (Hoppringle)	SG	SC	17th	Armagh, Down, Tyrone	-	-		-	-
	Prior	IG	-	-	Cavan, Leitrim	prior	IG		-	-
	Prior	NR	EN	-	Armagh, Down, Fermanagh, Longford, Louth, Monaghan	friar	NF		-	-

* see definitions

Prefix	Surname and Variation	Name Origin*	Migrated From*	Century Estab.	Geographical Locations	Definition of Surname	Language Origin*	Prefix	Pseudonyms and Synonyms	Name Origin*
	Proctor	EN	EN	17th	Antrim, Armagh, Down	-	-		-	-
(O)	Proudfoot	IG	-	-	Cork, Meath	-	-		-	-
	Prunty (Pronty, Bronte)	IG	-	-	Armagh, Down	bestower, generous person	IG		-	-
	Punch	NF	EN	13th	Armagh, Kildare, Munster	derived from Pontius	NF		-	-
	Purcell	NF	EN	-	Tipperary	little pig	NF		-	-
	Purdy	FR	-	17th	Ulster	-	-		-	-
	Pyke (Pike)	EN	EN	14th	Tipperary, Waterford	-	-		-	-
	Pyne	EN	EN	16th	Cork	-	-		-	-
	Pyper	GE	-	-	Limerick	-	-		-	-
	Piper	EN	-	-	Ulster	-	-		-	-
Mac	Quaid (-Quade)	IG	-	-	Limerick, Monaghan	son of Wat	IG		-	-
(O)	Quane (Quan, Quain)	IG	-	-	Sligo, Waterford	derived from the forename Cuan	IG		-	-
Mac	Quarrie	SG	SC	-	Ulster	noble	SG		-	-
	Quarry	FR	-	-	Cork, Waterford	squarely built	FR		-	-
Mac	Queen	SG	SC	-	Ulster	pleasant	SG	(Mac)	Quinn	IG
(O)	Queenan (Cunnane)	IG	-	-	Roscommon, Sligo	-	-		-	-
Mac	Queeney	IG	-	-	Clare, Roscommon	pleasant	IG	Mac	Weeney	IG
									Mulqueeney	IG
									Maqueeney	IG
	Quick	EN	EN	-	Cork	-	-		-	-

* see definitions

Prefix	Surname and Variation	Name Origin*	Migrated From*	Century Estab.	Geographical Locations	Definition of Surname	Language Origin*	Prefix	Pseudonyms and Synonyms	Name Origin*
(O)	Quigg	IG	-	-	Derry, Monaghan	five	IG		Fivey	EN
(O)	Quigley (Quig(g), Cogely, Kegley)	IG	-	-	Derry, Donegal Mayo, Meath, Wexford	-	-		-	-
(Mac)	Quilkin (- Culkin, (Culkeen)	IG	-	-	Galway	-	-		-	-
(O)	Quill	IG	-	-	Cork, Kerry	hazel	IG		Woods	EN
Mac	Quillan (- Cullen)	IG	-	-	Antrim	holly	IG	Mac	William Cullen	SG IG
(O)	Quillegan (Culligan)	IG	-	-	Clare, Limerick, Tipperary	-	IG	Mac	-	-
Mac	Quilly (- Gilly, Magilly)	IG	-	-	Monaghan, Roscommon	cock	IG		Cox	EN
	Quilter	NF	EN	-	Kerry	maker of quilts	NF		-	-
(O)	Quilty (Kiglty, Keeltagh, Keelty, Kielt)	IG	-	-	Connacht, Munster, Ulster	-	-		-	-
(O)	Quinlan (Conlan, Connellan, Kindellan)	IG	-	-	Leinster, Munster	gracefully shaped	IG		-	-
(O)	Quinlavin	IG	-	-	Clare	gracefully shaped	IG		Grimes	EN
(O)	Quinlish (Quinlisk, Conliss, Cunlish)	IG	-	-	Connacht, Tipperary	-	-		-	-
(O)	Quin(n) (Quinny)	IG	-	-	Antrim, Clare, Longford, Tyrone	intelligent	IG		-	-
	Quinnell	EN	EN	11th	Cork, Tipperary	woman-war	EN		-	-
(O)	Quinney (Cunny, Quinn)	IG	-	-	Sligo, Tyrone	derived from the forename Cannice or Kenny	IG		-	-

* see definitions

Prefix	Surname and Variation	Name Origin*	Migrated From*	Century Estab.	Geographical Locations	Definition of Surname	Language Origin*	Prefix	Pseudonyms and Synonyms	Name Origin*
	Quinton (Quentin)	FR	-	14th	Not closely identified with any particular locality	derived from St. Quentin	FR		-	-
(O)	Quirke (Kirke, Quick)	IG	-	-	Tipperary	heart	IG		Kirke Oates Quick	EN EN EN
	Quish (Cush)	IG	-	-	Cork, Laois, Limerick, Tipperary	-	-		-	-
Mac	Quiston (- Question, - Cutcheson)	SG	SC	-	Down	-	-		Houston	SG
	Rabbitt(e)	EN	EN	-	Clare, Galway, Mayo, Offaly	-	-		-	-
	Rabinovitch	JE	EE	-	Dublin	-	-		-	-
(O)	Ractigan (Radigan)	IG	-	-	Connacht	decree	IG		-	-
(O)	Rafferty (O' Roarty)	IG	-	-	Donegal, Louth, Tyrone	prosperity wielder	IG		-	-
(O)	Raftery	IG	-	-	Kilkenny, Mayo	decree	IG		-	-
(O)	Ragget	NF	EN	-	Kilkenny	untidy	IG		-	-
(O)	Raghteen	IG	-	-	Galway	decree	IG		-	-
(O)	Rahilly	IG	-	-	Munster, Ulster	-	IG		-	-
(O)	Rainey	EN	EN	-	Ulster	-	IG		Rawley	EN
Mac	Rankin	SG	SC	17th	Derry	diminutive of Randolph	SG		-	-
	Rannall	IG	-	-	Leitrim, Wexford	akin to Reginald	IG		Reynolds	EN
	Rath	NF	EN	-	Derry, Louth	-	-		-	-

* see definitions

Prefix	Surname and Variation	Name Origin*	Migrated From*	Century Estab.	Geographical Locations	Definition of Surname	Language Origin*	Prefix	Pseudonyms and Synonyms	Name Origin*
(O)	Ratigan (Rhatigan, Ractigan, Rattican)	IG	-	-	Roscommon	decree	IG		-	-
	Rawley (Raleigh)	EN	EN	16th	Limerick	-	-		-	-
(O)	Rea (Ray, MacRea)	IG	-	-	Antrim	property	IG		Wray	EN
(O)	Reaney	IG	-	-	Westmeath	a form of Reginald	IG		Rainey	EN
(O)	Reavey	IG	-	-	Down	grey or brindled	IG		Ray	EN
(O)	Redahan (Rodahan, Rudican, Roddy)	IG	-	-	Clare, Leitrim, Longford, Mayo	-	-		Reddington	EN
(O)	Reddan	IG	-	-	Clare	-	-		-	-
	Reddington	EN	EN	-	Galway, Mayo	-	-		-	-
(O)	Reddy	IG	-	-	Kilkenny	-	-		-	-
	Redmond	NF	EN	-	Wexford	-	-		-	-
Mac	Redmond	NF	EN	-	Galway, Offaly	-	-		-	-
	Reeves (Ryves)	EN	EN	17th	Down	-	-		-	-
(O)	Regan (Reagan)	IG	-	-	Clare, Cork, Laois, Waterford	-	-		-	-
	Reid (Reade)	EN	EN	-	Ulster	red	EN		-	-
(O)	Reidy	IG	-	-	Clare, Kerry, Tipperary	driving or career	IG		-	-
(O)	Reighill (Rehill, Reehill, Rahill, Reckle)	IG	-	-	Cavan, Kerry, Longford	-	-		-	-

* see definitions

Prefix	Surname and Variation	Name Origin*	Migrated From*	Century Estab.	Geographical Locations	Definition of Surname	Language Origin*	Prefix	Pseudonyms and Synonyms	Name Origin*
(O)	Reilly	IG	-	-	Cavan, Meath	-	-		-	-
(O)	Relahan	IG	-	-	Antrim, Cork, Kerry	-	-		-	-
(O)	Renehan (Ronaghan)	IG	-	-	Cork, Monaghan, Offaly	sharp-pointed, starry	IG		Ferns	EN
	Rennick (Renwick, Rennix)	EN	EN	16th	Kildare, Meath, Monaghan	-	-		-	-
	Reville	FR	EN	17th	Wexford	-	-		-	-
	Rice	WE	-	-	Munster	-	-		-	-
	Rhys	IG	-	-	Armagh, Down, Fermanagh, Louth, Monaghan	-	-		-	-
	Richards	EN	EN	-	Ulster	-	-		-	-
	Richardson	EN	EN	-	Ulster	-	-		-	-
	Ridgeway	EN	EN	16th	Laois, Ulster, Waterford	-	-		-	-
(O)	Rigney	IG	-	-	Offaly	-	-		-	-
(O)	Riney	IG	-	-	Kerry	-	-		-	-
(O)	Ring	IG	-	-	Cork	spear	IG		Wrenn	EN
	Ringrose	EN	EN	17th	Clare	-	-		-	-
(Mac)	Rinn	IG	-	-	Leitrim	raven	IG	Mac	Crann	IG
(O)	Riordan (Rearden)	IG	-	-	Cork	royal bard	IG		-	-
(Mac)	Ritchie	SG	SC	-	Ulster	diminutive of Richard	SG		-	-
	Roan (Rowan)	EN	EN	-	Roscommon	-	-		-	-

* see definitions

Prefix	Surname and Variation	Name Origin*	Migrated From*	Century Estab.	Geographical Locations	Definition of Surname	Language Origin*	Prefix	Pseudonyms and Synonyms	Name Origin*
(Mac)	Roarty	IG	-	-	Donegal	prosperity weilder	IG		-	-
(Mac)	Robb	SG	SC	-	Ulster	-	-		Grubb	EN
	Roberts	IG	-	-	All Provinces	-	-		-	-
Mac	Roberts	SG	SC	-	Ulster	-	-		-	-
	Robinson	EN	EN	-	Ulster	-	EN		-	-
	Robson	EN	EN	-	Ulster	son of Rob	-		-	-
	Roche	NF	EN	-	Cork, Kilkenny, Wexford	rock	NF		-	-
	Rochford	NF	EN	-	Kilkenny, Meath	-	-		-	-
	Rock	EN	EN	-	Clare, Leitrim, Sligo	-	-		-	-
(O)	Rodden (Roden, Ruden)	IG	-	-	Cavan, Donegal	strong	IG		-	-
(O)	Roddy	IG	-	-	Donegal, Leitrim	-	-		-	-
(O)	Roe	IG	-	-	Waterford	red	IG		-	-
(O)	Rogan	IG	-	-	Armagh, Leitrim	red	IG		-	-
(O)	Rodgers (Rogers)	EN	EN	-	All Provinces	-	-		-	-
(O)	Rohan	IG	-	-	Cork, Kerry	-	-		Rowan	EN
(O)	Ronan (Ronayne)	IG	-	-	Cork, Dublin, Mayo	a seal	IG		-	-
(O)	Rooke	EN	EN	-	Leitrim	a bird	EN		-	-
(O)	Rooneen (Roonian)	IG	-	-	Donegal, Leitrim, Sligo	-	-		-	-
(O)	Rooney	IG	-	-	Connacht, Leinster, Ulster	-	-		-	-

* see definitions

Prefix	Surname and Variation	Name Origin*	Migrated From*	Century Estab.	Geographical Locations	Definition of Surname	Language Origin*	Prefix	Pseudonyms and Synonyms	Name Origin*
Mac	Rory	IG	-	-	Derry, Tyrone	-	-		Rodgers Rogers	EN
	Rose	EN	EN	17th	Limerick	shrub or flower	EN		-	-
	Roseman (Rosemond)	GE	EN	17th	Cavan, Leitrim	-	-		-	-
	Ross	SG	SC	-	Uslter	-	-		Andrew	IG
	Ross	EN	EN	-	Cork, Dublin	-	-		-	-
	Rossiter	EN	EN	-	Wexford	-	-		-	-
	Rothe (Routh)	NS	-	14th	Kilkenny	red	NS		-	-
	Rountree (Roantree, Roundtree, Rowantree)	EN	EN	14th	Armagh, Cavan	a rowan tree	EN		-	-
(O)	Rourke	IG	-	-	Leitrim	-	-		Rooke	EN
	Rowan	EN	EN	-	Galway, Mayo, Cork, Kerry	a rowan tree	EN		-	-
	Roy	FR	EN	-	Dulbin	king	FR		Ray	EN
	Roycroft (Raycraft, Raecraft, Royse)	EN	EN	17th	Cork	rye croft	EN		-	-
(O)	Ruane (Royan)	IG	-	-	Galway, Mayo	red	IG		Rowan	EN
	Ruby	FR	-	17th	Cork	-	-		-	-
	Rudd	EN	EN	17th	Wexford	red	EN		-	-
	Ruddle (Ruddell)	EN	EN	13th	Armagh, Kerry, Leinster, Limerick	-	-		-	-

* see definitions

Prefix	Surname and Variation	Name Origin*	Migrated From*	Century Estab.	Geographical Locations	Definition of Surname	Language Origin*	Prefix	Pseudonyms and Synonyms	Name Origin*
Mac	Ruddery	IG	-	-	Westmeath	knight	IG	Mac	Knight	IG
(O)	Rush	IG	-	-	Mayo, Monaghan	wood	IG		-	-
	Russell	FR	EN	12th	Leinster, Ulster	a red-haired person	FR		Rossel	FR
	Ruttle (Ruckle)	GE	-	-	Limerick	-	-		Ruddle	EN
	Rutledge	EN	EN	17th	Fermanagh, Mayo, Tyrone	-	-		-	-
(O)	Ryan (Mulryan)	IG	-	-	Carlow, Tipperary	-	-		-	-
	Ryder	EN	EN	-	Clare, Louth, Monaghan	-	-		-	-
(O)	Ryle (Riall)	IG	-	-	Kerry	-	-		-	-
(Mac)	Rynne	IG	-	-	Clare, Connacht	raven	IG	Mac	Crann	IG
	Sadlier (Sadleir)	EN	EN	16th	Cork, Dublin	-	-		-	-
	St. Clair	NF	EN	-	Ulster	-	-		Sinclair	SG
	St. John (Singen)	NF	EN	13th	Tipperary, Wexford	-	-		-	-
	St. Lawrence	NF	EN	12th	Clare, Dublin	-	-		-	-
	St. Leger	NF	EN	14th	Kilkenny	-	-		Ledger Sallenger	GE FR
	Salmon	EN	EN	16th	Kilkenny, Laois	-	-		-	-
	Salmon (Sammon, Bradden)	IG	-	-	Clare, Donegal, Leitrim	-	-		Fisher	EN
	Sampson	EN	EN	14th	Leinster, Munster	-	-		-	-

* see definitions

Prefix	Surname and Variation	Name Origin*	Migrated From*	Century Estab.	Geographical Locations	Definition of Surname	Language Origin*	Prefix	Pseudonyms and Synonyms	Name Origin*
	Sand[e]s (Sandys)	EN	EN	16th	Munster, Ulster	sand	EN		-	-
	Sarsfield	NF	EN	12th	Cork, Dublin, Kildare, Limerick	-	-		-	-
	Saurin	NF	EN	-	Cavan, Meath, Monaghan, Tyrone	-	-		Soden	EN
	Savage	NF	NR	13th	Down, Kilkenny	fierce person	NF		Sage	NF
O	Savin	IG	-	-	Munster	strong, firm	IG		Savage	NF
	Sayers	EN	EN	-	Kerry, Ulster	-	-		-	-
(O)	Scallan	IG	-	-	Fermanagh, Wexford	kernel	IG		-	-
(Mac)	Scally (Miskelly)	IG	-	-	Roscommon, Westmeath	student	IG		-	-
(Mac)	Scanlan	IG	-	-	Louth	contention	IG		-	-
(O)	Scanlan (Scannell)	IG	-	-	Clare, Cork, Fermanagh, Galway	contention	IG		-	-
(O)	Scannell (Scanlan)	IG	-	-	Sligo	contention	IG		-	-
(O)	Scarry (Scurry)	IG	-	-	Galway, Kilkenny, Waterford	-	-		-	-
Mac	Scollog	IG	-	-	Monaghan	farmer	IG		Farmer	EN
	Scott	EN	EN	-	Dublin, Ulster	-	-		-	-
(O)	Scullin (Scullane, Scullion, Skoolin)	IG	-	-	Derry	-	-	(O)	Scully	IG
(O)	Scully	IG	-	-	Tipperary, Westmeath	student	IG		-	-
	Seaver	EN	EN	17th	Armagh, Monaghan	sea-passage	EN		-	-

Prefix	Surname and Variation	Name Origin*	Migrated From*	Century Estab.	Geographical Locations	Definition of Surname	Language Origin*	Prefix	Pseudonyms and Synonyms	Name Origin*
(O)	Seery	IG	-	-	Westmeath	-	-		Freeman	EN
									Earner	EN
	Semple	SG	SC	17th	Ulster	simple	SG		-	-
	Semple	FR	EN	-	Ulster	St. Pol	FR		-	-
	Sergeant	EN	EN	-	Armagh	-	-		-	-
	Seward (Seaward)	EN	EN	17th	Cork	-	-		-	-
	Sewell	EN	EN	-	Cork	-	-		-	-
	Sexton (Shasnan)	IG	-	-	Limerick	quick-eyed	EN		Tackney	EN
	Seymour	FR	EN	17th	Armagh, Cork	-	-		Emo	EN
	Shackleton	EN	EN	18th	Kildare	-	-		-	-
(O)	Shalley (Shalvey, Shalloo, Shallow)	IG	-	-	Cork	having possesions	IG		Shelly	EN
	Shamrock	EN	EN	16th	Cork, Waterford	-	-		Hamrock	EN
(Mac)	Shanaghy	IG	-	-	Connacht	storyteller	IG		Fox	EN
(Mac)	Shanahan (Shannon)	IG	-	-	Clare	old	IG		Johnson	SG
(Mac)	Shane	IG	-	-	Kerry, Louth, Tyrone, Westmeath	-	-		Johnson	SG
(Mac)	Shanley	IG	-	-	Leitrim	old hero	IG		-	-
	Shannon	IG	-	-	All Provinces	wise	IG		-	-
(O)	Sharkey	IG	-	-	Louth, Ulster	loving	IG		-	-
	Sharpe	EN	EN	-	Donegal	sharp	EN		-	-

* see definitions

Prefix	Surname and Variation	Name Origin*	Migrated From*	Century Estab.	Geographical Locations	Definition of Surname	Language Origin*	Prefix	Pseudonyms and Synonyms	Name Origin*
(Mac)	Sharry	IG	-	-	Leitrim, Roscommon	foal, flighty	IG	(O)	Foley	IG
(O)	Sharry	IG	-	-	Ulster	foal, flighty	IG		-	-
(O)	Shaughnessy	IG	-	-	Galway	-	-		Sands	EN
	Shaw	SG	SC	16th	Dublin, Ulster	-	-		-	-
(O)	Shea (Shee)	IG	-	-	Kerry, Kilkenny, Tipperary	hawklike, stately	IG		-	-
	Shearman (Sharman)	EN	EN	17th	Dublin, Kilkenny	-	-		-	-
(Mac)	Sheedy	IG	-	-	Clare	silken, soft-spoken	IG	Mac	Namara	IG
(O)	Sheedy	IG	-	-	Clare, Galway	silken, soft-spoken	IG		Silke	EN
(O)	Sheehan (Sheahan)	IG	-	-	Cork, Kerry, Limerick	-	-		-	-
(Mac)	Sheehy	SG	SC	-	Limerick	eerie	SG		-	-
(O)	Sheenan	IG	-	-	Monaghan, Tyrone	-	-		-	-
(O)	Sheeran (Sheerin)	IG	-	-	Donegal, Fermanagh, Laois	-	-		-	-
	Sheldon	EN	EN	-	Ulster	-	-		-	-
	Sheppard (Shepherd)	EN	EN	13th	Leinster, Munster, Ulster	-	-		-	-
(Mac)	Shera (Sheera)	IG	-	-	Kilkenny	an equivalent of Geoffrey	IG		-	-
(O)	Sheridan	IG	-	-	Cavan, Longford	-	-		-	-
	Sherlock (Scurlock)	EN	EN	-	Meath, Westmeath	short-haired	EN		-	-
	Sherman (Shearman, Sharmin)	EN	EN	18th	Dublin, Kilkenny	-	-		-	-

* see definitions

Prefix	Surname and Variation	Name Origin*	Migrated From*	Century Estab.	Geographical Locations	Definition of Surname	Language Origin*	Prefix	Pseudonyms and Synonyms	Name Origin*
(Mac)	Sherry	IG	-	-	Armagh, Cork	foal	IG		-	-
	Sherwin (Sharvin, Sharvan)	IG	-	-	Roscommon	bitter	IG		-	-
	Sherwin	EN	EN	-	Dublin, Ulster	-	-		-	-
	Sherwood	EN	EN	17th	All Provinces	-	-		-	-
(O)	Shevlin	IG	-	-	Donegal, Mayo, Monaghan, Offaly	swift	IG		-	-
(O)	Shiel (Shields)	IG	-	-	Donegal, Offaly, Ulster	-	-		-	-
(O)	Shine	IG	-	-	Cork, Kerry	small hawk	IG		-	-
(O)	Shinnagh (Shinagh, Shunagh)	IG	-	-	Galway, Mayo	-	-	(O)	Fox / Shinnick / Shunny	EN / IG / IG
(O)	Shinnick (Shinnock)	IG	-	-	Cork	fox	IG		-	-
	Shire (Shier)	GE	-	-	Limerick	-	-		-	-
	Short	EN	EN	-	Dublin, Ulster	-	-		-	-
	Shortall	EN	EN	13th	Kilkenny	short neck	EN		-	-
	Silke	EN	EN	-	Galway	-	-		-	-
	Simms	SG	SC	17th	Antrim, Donegal	pet name for Simon	SG		-	-
	Singleton	EN	EN	14th	Cork, Louth, Monaghan	-	-		-	-
	Sinnott	EN	EN	13th	Wexford	victory - bold	EN		-	-
(O)	Skallen	IG	-	-	Fermanagh	-	-		-	-
	Skeffington	EN	EN	16th	Connacht, Ulster	-	-		-	-

* see definitions

Prefix	Surname and Variation	Name Origin*	Migrated From*	Century Estab.	Geographical Locations	Definition of Surname	Language Origin*	Prefix	Pseudonyms and Synonyms	Name Origin*
(Mac)	Skehan	IG	-	-	Louth, Monaghan, Tipperary	briar	IG		Thornton	EN
	Skelton	EN	EN	15th	Dublin, Laois, Ulster	-	-		-	-
	Skerett	EN	EN	13th	Galway	-	-		-	-
	Skiddy	NS	SC	14th	Cork	-	-		-	-
	Slamon	IG	-	-	Ulster	-	-	(O)	Slevin	IG
	Slater (Slator, Sleater)	EN SG	EN SC	-	Dublin, Longford Louth	-	-		-	-
(O)	Slattery	IG	-	-	Clare	strong	IG		-	-
(O)	Slavin (Slevin)	IG	-	-	Fermanagh, Westmeath	mountain	IG		-	-
(Mac)	Sleyne (Sliney)	IG	-	-	Cork	-	IG		-	-
(O)	Sloan(e) (Sloyan)	IG	-	-	Antrim, Armagh, Down, Mayo	hosting or army	IG		-	-
(Mac)	Slowey (Sloy, Molloy)	IG	-	-	Cavan, Monaghan	hosting or army	IG	(O)	Molloy	IG
	Small	EN	EN	-	Galway, Ulster	-	-		-	-
	Smith (Smyth)	EN	EN	-	Cavan	-	-		-	-
(O)	Snee	IG	-	-	Mayo	-	-		-	-
	Snoddy (Snoddie)	SG	SC	-	Carlow	-	-		-	-
	Snow	EN	EN	16th	Ulster	-	-		-	-
	Soden (Soudan)	EN	EN	17th	Cavan, Meath, Sligo	sultan	EN		-	-

* see definitions

Prefix	Surname and Variation	Name Origin*	Migrated From*	Century Estab.	Geographical Locations	Definition of Surname	Language Origin*	Prefix	Pseudonyms and Synonyms	Name Origin*
(Mac)	Solly	IG	-	-	Louth, Monaghan	-	-		-	-
(O)	Somahan	IG	-	-	Cork, Sligo, Ulster	soft, innocent person	IG		Somers Summers Somerville	EN EN EN
	Somers (Summers)	EN	EN	-	Leinster	-	-		-	-
	Somerville (Sumeril, Summerly)	EN	EN	-	Cork, Ulster	-	-		-	-
(O)	Sorahan	IG	-	-	Cavan, Monaghan	bright	IG		Saurin	NF
Mac	Sorley	NS	SC	-	Antrim, Tyrone	-	-		-	-
Mac	Spadden	IG	-	-	Down	-	-		Spedding	EN
	Spaight	EN	EN	17th	Clare, Limerick	woodpecker	EN		-	-
Mac	Sparran (- Asparran)	SG	SC	-	Antrim, Derry	purse	SG		-	-
	Sparrow	EN	EN	17th	Wexford	a bird, flutterer	EN		-	-
	Spelman	IG	-	-	Sligo	-	-		-	-
	Spence	SG	SC	-	Antrim, Down	-	-		-	-
	Spenser	EN	EN	-	Leinster	-	-		-	-
(Mac)	Spillane (Splaine)	IG	-	-	Offaly	scythe	IG		Spelman Spenser	IG EN
	Spring	EN	EN	16th	Kerry	-	-		-	-
	Stacey	NF	EN	-	Wexford, Wicklow	diminutive of Eustace	NF		-	-
	Stack	EN	EN	13th	Kerry	a stack	EN		-	-
	Stacpoole	IG	-	-	Clare	foreigner, black	IG		-	-

* see definitions

Prefix	Surname and Variation	Name Origin*	Migrated From*	Century Estab.	Geographical Locations	Definition of Surname	Language Origin*	Prefix	Pseudonyms and Synonyms	Name Origin*
(O)	Conrahy (Conroy)	IG	-	-	Laois, Offaly	-	-		-	-
(O)	Conroy (Conree, Conary, Conry)	IG	-	-	Clare, Galway, Roscommon	hound of prosperity	IG		King	EN
(Mac)	Considine	IG	-	-	Clare	-	-		-	-
Mac	Consnave	IG	-	-	Leitrim	-	-		-	-
Mac	Conville (- Conwell)	IG	-	-	Armagh, Down, Louth	-	-		-	-
Mac	Conway (Conboy, Convey, Mac Conaway)	IG	-	-	Clare, Limerick, Mayo Sligo, Tipperary, Tyrone	head smashing	IG		-	-
Mac	Conwell	IG	-	-	Donegal	-	-	Mac	Conville	IG
(O)	Coogan	IG	-	-	Galway, Kilkenny, Monaghan	-	-		Cogan Cogan	WE WE
	Cooke	EN	EN	-	Leinster	cook	EN		-	-
	Cooke (Mac Cooge, Mac Hugo)	IG	-	-	Connacht	-	-		-	-
Mac	Cook (-Cuagh)	SG	SC	-	Ulster	-	-		Cogan Cogan	WE WE
(Mac)	Cool	IG	-	-	Donegal	devotee of St. Comaghal	IG		Cole	EN
	Coolahan	IG	-	-	Mayo	-	-		-	-
(O)	Cooley (Cowley, Colley)	IG	-	-	Clare, Galway, Ulster	-	-		-	-
(O)	Coonan (Conan)	IG	-	-	Offaly, Sligo, Tipperary	elegant	IG		-	-

* see definitions

Prefix	Surname and Variation	Name Origin*	Migrated From*	Century Estab.	Geographical Locations	Definition of Surname	Language Origin*	Prefix	Pseudonyms and Synonyms	Name Origin*
	Studdert	EN	EN	17th	Clare	keeper of horses	EN		-	-
	Stuppel	JE	EE	-	Dublin	-	-		-	-
(O)	Sugrue (Shugrue)	NS	NS	-	Kerry	-	-		-	-
(O)	Sullivan	IG	-	-	Cork, Kerry, Tipperary	-	IG		-	-
(O)	Sully	IG	-	-	Leinster, Munster	student	-		-	-
	Sutton	NF	EN	13th	Kildare, Wexford	-	-		-	-
	Swayne	NS	EN	13th	Leinster	servant	NS		-	-
(Mac)	Sweeney (Swiney)	IG	-	-	Cork, Donegal, Kerry	pleasant	IG		-	-
	Sweetman	NS	NS	12th	Kilkenny	-	-		-	-
	Sweetnam	EN	EN	-	Cork	-	-		Sweetnam	EN
	Swift	EN	EN	17th	Mayo	-	-		-	-
Mac	Swiggan	NS	-	-	Tyrone	-	-		-	-
	Swords	IG	-	-	Dublin, Laois, Offaly	-	-		-	-
	Sydes (Scythes, Sides)	EN	EN	-	Dublin, Kilkenny	dweller by the slopes	EN		-	-
	Synan (Synon)	NF	EN	13th	Cork	-	-		-	-
	Synge (Sing)	EN	EN	17th	Cork, Dublin, Louth, Offaly, Wicklow	-	-		-	-
	Taaff (Taa)	WE	-	13th	Louth, Sligo	son of David	WE		-	-
	Tackney	EN	EN	-	Cavan	-	-		-	-

* see definitions

Prefix	Surname and Variation	Name Origin*	Migrated From*	Century Estab.	Geographical Locations	Definition of Surname	Language Origin*	Prefix	Pseudonyms and Synonyms	Name Origin*
(O)	Tagan (Teegan)	IG	-	-	Kildare, Laois	from the forename Teigue	IG		-	-
Mac	Taghlin	IG	-	-	Donegal	devotee of St. Seachlainn	IG		Houston	SG
(O)	Taheny (Teahan)	IG	EN	-	Roscommon	fugitive	IG		-	-
	Talbot	NF	-	12th	Dublin	-	-		-	-
(O)	Tally	IG	EN	-	Fermanagh, Longford	peaceable	IG	(Mac)	Tully	IG
	Tandy	EN	EN	14th	Meath	a pet name for Andrew	EN		-	-
	Tanner	NF	EN	-	Laois	-	-		-	-
	Tarleton	EN	EN	17th	Offaly	-	-		-	-
(O)	Tarpey	IG	-	-	Connacht, Cork, Sligo	sturdy	IG		-	-
	Tarrant	EN	EN	-	Cork	-	-		Thornton	EN
Mac	Tavish	SG	SC	-	Cavan	-	-		Thomson Thompson	SG EN
	Taylor	EN	EN	14th	Dublin, Ulster	-	-		-	-
(O)	Teahan (Tehan, Teehan)	IG	-	-	Kerry, Kilkenny, Tipperary	fugitive	IG		-	-
(O)	Teevan	IG	-	-	Fermanagh, Monaghan	-	-		-	-
Mac	Teige (- Tigue)	IG	-	-	Donegal, Galway, Mayo, Monaghan	-	-	Mac	Montague Cague Caig	NF IG IG
	Tempest	EN	EN	17th	Louth, Ulster	-	-		-	-
Mac	Ternan (Tiernan)	IG	-	-	Cavan, Leitrim	lord	IG		-	-
	Terry	FR	EN	13th	Cork	people rule	GE		-	-

* see definitions

Prefix	Surname and Variation	Name Origin*	Migrated From*	Century Estab.	Geographical Locations	Definition of Surname	Language Origin*	Prefix	Pseudonyms and Synonyms	Name Origin*
(O)	Tevlin	IG	-	-	Cavan, Meath	-	-		-	-
	Tew	EN	EN	16th	Meath, Waterford	-	-		-	-
	Thackaberry (Tackaberry)	EN	EN	17th	Wexford, Wicklow	-	-		-	-
	Thomas	EN	EN	-	Antrim, Down, Dublin	-	-		-	-
	Thom(p)son	EN	EN	-	Ulster	-	-		-	-
	Thomson	SG	SC	-	Ulster	-	-		-	-
	Thornhill	EN	EN	17th	Cork, Limerick	-	-		-	-
	Thornton (Thorne)	EN	EN	-	Limerick	-	-		-	-
(O)	Thynne (O'Tyne)	IG	-	-	Clare	dusk or gloom	IG		-	-
(O)	Tierney	IG	-	-	Donegal, Mayo, Westmeath	lord	IG		Lord	EN
	Tiffeny	EN	EN	-	Leitrim	epiphany	EN		-	-
(Mac)	Timlin (Tomilin, Tomlin)	NF	EN	17th	Mayo	diminutive of Thomas	NF		-	-
	Timmon (Timon)	IG	-	-	Carlow, Mayo, Wicklow	short name for Thomas	IG		-	-
(O)	Timon (Timmons, Tymon)	IG	-	-	Mayo	-	-		-	-
	Timothy	EN	EN	-	Galway, Roscommon	-	-		-	-
Mac	Timpany	IG	-	-	Derry, Down	tympanist (musician)	IG		-	-
	Tinsley (Townsley)	EN	EN	-	Kildare	-	-		-	-

* see definitions

Prefix	Surname and Variation	Name Origin*	Migrated From*	Century Estab.	Geographical Locations	Definition of Surname	Language Origin*	Prefix	Pseudonyms and Synonyms	Name Origin*
	Tipper	EN	EN	14th	Kildare	-	-		-	-
	Tobin	NF	EN	-	Kilkenny, Tipperary	-	-		-	-
(O)	Tolan[d] (Toolan)	IG	-	-	Mayo, Ulster	people mighty	IG		-	-
	Toler (Toller)	EN	EN	17th	Leitrim, Tipperary	tax gatherer	FR		-	-
(O)	Tolleran	IG	-	-	Mayo	obstinate	IG		-	-
(O)	Toman (Tooman)	IG	-	-	Roscommon, Tyrone	-	-		-	-
	Tone	EN	EN	16th	Dublin	enclosure, village	EN		-	-
(O)	Toner (Tonry)	IG	-	-	Armagh, Derry, Donegal	-	-		-	-
(O)	Toole	IG	-	-	Kildare, Mayo, Wicklow	people mighty	IG		-	-
(O)	Toorish (Houriskey, Horish)	IG	-	-	Donegal	things	IG		Tidings Waters	EN EN
	Tormey	NS	-	-	Cavan, Longford, Westmeath	-	-		-	-
(O)	Torney	IG	-	-	Cork, Kerry, Ulster	-	-		-	-
	Tottenham	EN	EN	17th	Wexford	-	-		-	-
(O)	Tougher (Tooher)	IG	-	-	Connacht, Ulster	people dear	IG		Tucker	EN
	Townsend (Townshend)	EN	EN	17th	Cork	-	-		-	-
(O)	Tracey (Treacy)	IG	-	-	All provinces	war-like	IG		-	-

* see definitions

Prefix	Surname and Variation	Name Origin*	Migrated From*	Century Estab.	Geographical Locations	Definition of Surname	Language Origin*	Prefix	Pseudonyms and Synonyms	Name Origin*
(Mac)	Traynor (Treanor)	IG	-	-	Armagh, Down, Fermanagh, Louth, Monaghan	strong man	IG		Armstong Cramer Creamer	EN GE EN
	Trench	FR	-	17th	Galway, Laois	-	-		-	-
(O)	Trohy (Troy)	IG	-	-	Clare, Kilkenny, Tipperary	foot soldier	IG		-	-
(O)	Trower	IG	-	-	Letrim	skilful	IG		Treyor	EN
	Tucker	EN	EN	-	Connacht, Ulster	-	-		-	-
(Mac)	Tully (Mac Atilla)	IG	-	-	Cavan, Longford	flood	IG		Flood	EN
(Mac)	Tumelty	IG	-	-	Down, Louth, Monaghan, Roscommon	bulky	IG		Timothy	EN
(O)	Tunney	IG	-	-	Donegal, Mayo, Sligo	billowy, wave, glittering	IG		-	-
(O)	Tuohy	IG	-	-	Clare, Galway	ruler	IG		Tutty	EN
(Mac)	Turley (Torley)	IG	-	-	Armagh, Down	-	-		Terry	FR
	Turner (MacInturner)	EN SG	EN SC	15th 15th	All provinces	-	-		-	-
	Tweedy (Tweedie)	SG	SC	17th	Ulster	-	-		-	-
	Twiss	EN	EN	-	Kerry	dweller by the bend in the road	EN		-	-
(O)	Twomey (Toomey)	IG	-	-	Cork, Kerry, Limerick	-	-		-	-
(O)	Tynan (Tinnan)	IG	-	-	Connacht, Laois	dark or grey	IG		-	-

* see definitions

Prefix	Surname and Variation	Name Origin*	Migrated From*	Century Estab.	Geographical Locations	Definition of Surname	Language Origin*	Prefix	Pseudonyms and Synonyms	Name Origin*
	Ultagh	IG	-	-	Westmeath	Ulsterman	IG		North	EN
	Unehan (Oonihan)	IG	-	-	Carlow	-	-		-	-
	Uniacke	IG	-	-	Cork	-	-		Garde	EN
	Uprichard	WE	-	-	Armagh	-	-		Pritchard	EN
	Upton	EN	EN	16th	Antrim, Cork	-	-		-	-
	Ussher (Lush)	NF	EN	14th	Dublin, Galway, Waterford	-	-		-	-
(Mac)	Vaddock	IG	-	-	Wexford	-	-		-	-
	Valentine	LA	EN	17th	Wicklow	strong	LA		-	-
	Vallelly (Vally)	IG	-	-	Armagh, Monaghan	-	-		-	-
	Vance	EN	EN	17th	Ulster	-	EN		-	-
(Mac)	Varrelly	IG	-	-	Connacht	marsh or fen	IG		-	-
	Vaugh	IG	-	-	Leitrim	sharp-eyed man	-		-	-
(Mac)	Vaughan	WE	-	16th	Clare	-	WE		-	-
	Veagh (-Veigh)	IG	-	-	Ulster	little	IG	Mac Mac	Evoy Vaugh Vesey	IG IG FR
	Veale (Vail)	NF	EN	-	Waterford	life	NF		Calfe	NF
	Veitch	SG	SC	-	Cavan, Fermanagh	calf	-		-	-
	Verdon	NF	EN	17th	Louth	-	-		-	-
	Vesey	FR	EN	-	Mayo	-	-		-	-

* see definitions

Prefix	Surname and Variation	Name Origin*	Migrated From*	Century Estab.	Geographical Locations	Definition of Surname	Language Origin*	Prefix	Pseudonyms and Synonyms	Name Origin*
Mac	Vicar (-Vicker)	SG	SC	-	Ulster	son of the Vicar	SG		-	-
	Vicars	SG	SC	16th	Laois	-	-		-	-
	Vickery	EN	EN	17th	Cork	agent	LA		-	-
	Vigors	FR	-	17th	Carlow	strong	FR		-	-
	Villiers	SG	SC	16th	Laois	-	-		-	-
	Vincent	EN	EN	17th	Dublin, Limerick	-	-		-	-
	Viniter	NF	EN	-	Cork	vintner	NF		-	-
Mac	Vitty	IG	-	-	Antrim	caterer	IG		-	-
	Wachman	JE	EE	-	Dublin	-	-		-	-
	Wade	EN	EN	13th	All Provinces	to go	EN		-	-
	Wade	NF	EN	13th	All Provinces	ford	NF		-	-
	Wafer (Weafer)	EN	EN	13th	Wexford	maker of eucharistic wafers	EN		-	-
	Walker	EN	EN	-	Dublin, Ulster	a fuller of clothes	EN		-	-
	Wall (Wale)	NF	EN	-	Limerick, Waterford	-	-		-	-
	Wallace (Wallis)	NF	EN	-	Ulster	the Welshman	NF		-	-
	Waller	EN	EN	17th	Limerick, Tipperary	-	-		-	-
	Walpole	EN	EN	17th	Laois, Leitirm	-	-		Wallace	-
	Walsh (Brannagh, Brannick, Welsh)	IG	-	-	All Provinces	Welshman	IG		-	NF

Prefix	Surname and Variation	Name Origin*	Migrated From*	Century Estab.	Geographical Locations	Definition of Surname	Language Origin*	Prefix	Pseudonyms and Synonyms	Name Origin*
	Walton	EN	EN	13th	Not closely associated with any specific area	-	-		-	-
(Mac)	Ward	EN	EN	-	Donegal, Galway	son of the Bard	IG		-	-
	Waring	NF	EN	13th	Down, Kilkenny, Meath	-	-		-	-
	Warner	EN	EN	17th	Cork	-	-		-	-
Mac	Warnock	IG	-	-	Down	devotee of St. Mearnog	IG		-	-
	Warren	FR	-	-	Kerry	-	-		-	-
	Waters	EN	EN	12th	Cork	water, Walter	EN		-	-
	Watkins	EN	EN	16th	Connacht	diminutive of Walter	EN		-	-
	Watson	SG	SC	-	Ulster	-	-		-	-
	Watson	EN	EN	-	Ulster	son of Wat (Walter)	EN		-	-
	Waugh	SG	SC	17th	All Provinces	foreigner	EN	Mac	Vaugh	IG
	Webb	EN	EN	17th	Antrim, Down, Dublin	-	-		-	-
	Webster	EN	EN	17th	Leinster, Ulster	weaver	EN		-	-
	Wedelesky	JE	EE	-	Dublin	-	-		-	-
Mac	Weeney	IG	-	-	Leitrim, Roscommon	wealth, dumb	IG		-	-
	Weiner	JE	EE	-	Dublin	-	-		-	-
	Weir (Weer)	IG	-	-	Armagh	steward	IG		-	-
	Weir	EN	EN	-	Westmeath	-	-		-	-
	Weir	SG	SC	16th	Ulster	-	-		-	-

* see definitions

Prefix	Surname and Variation	Name Origin*	Migrated From*	Century Estab.	Geographical Locations	Definition of Surname	Language Origin*	Prefix	Pseudonyms and Synonyms	Name Origin*
	Welby	EN	EN	-	Galway	-	-		-	-
	Weldon (Veldon, Beldon)	EN	EN	14th	Dublin	-	-		Belton Veldon	EN EN
	Weldon (Meldon)	IG	-	-	Fermanagh	-	-	(O)	Muldoon Meldon	IG IF
	Wells	EN	EN	13th	Leinster, Munster, Ulster	-	-		-	-
	Weston	NF	EN	17th	Leinster, Munster	-	-		-	-
(O)	Whearty	IG	-	-	Louth, Mayo, Westmeath	noisy	IG		-	-
	Wheeler	EN	EN	17th	Dublin, Kilkenny, Laois, Limerick	-	-		-	-
(O)	Whelan (Phelan)	IG	-	-	Tipperary, Ulster, Wexford	wolf	IG		-	-
	Whelehan (Helehan)	IG	-	-	Munster, Westmeath	joyful	IG	(O)	Whelan	IG
Mac	Whirter	SG	SC	-	Antrim, Armagh	son of the harper	SG		-	-
	Whitaker (Whiteacre)	EN	EN	14th	Louth, Meath	-	-		-	-
	White	EN	EN	14th	All Provinces	-	-		-	-
	Whitmore	EN	EN	17th	Dublin, Wexford	-	-		-	-
	Whitney	EN	EN	14th	Leinster	-	-		-	-
	Whitty (Whitey)	EN	EN	13th	Wexford	-	-		-	-
	Whooley (Wholey)	IG	-	-	Cork	boastful	IG		-	-
	Whoriskey	IG	-	-	Donegal	-	-		Waters	EN

* see definitions

Prefix	Surname and Variation	Name Origin*	Migrated From*	Century Estab.	Geographical Locations	Definition of Surname	Language Origin*	Prefix	Pseudonyms and Synonyms	Name Origin*
	Wickham (Wycomb)	EN	EN	14th	Connacht, Dublin, Wexford	-	-		-	-
	Wiggins	NF	EN	-	Fermanagh	-	-		-	-
	Wilde	EN	EN	18th	Mayo	-	-		-	-
	Williams	WE	-	-	All Provinces	-	-		-	-
Mac	William(s)	SG	SC	-	Ulster	-	-		-	-
	Williamson	SG	SC	-	Ulster	-	-		-	-
	Wilson	EN	EN	-	Ulster	-	-		-	-
	Winston	EN	EN	16th	Roscommon, Waterford	-	-		-	-
	Winters	EN	EN	-	Tyrone	winter	IG		-	-
	Wiseman	EN	EN	16th	Cork	-	-		-	-
	Wogan	WE	-	13th	Kildare	frown	WE		-	-
	Woodcock	EN	EN	13th	Dublin, Waterford	-	-		-	-
	Woodman	EN	EN	14th	Louth	-	-		-	-
	Woods	EN	EN	-	All Provinces	-	-		-	-
	Woolahan (Wolohan)	IG	-	-	Kilkenny, Wicklow	-	-		-	-
	Worth	EN	EN	17th	Leinster, Munster	homestead	EN		-	-
	Woulfe	NF	EN	-	Kildare, Limerick	-	-		Nix Wooley	EN IG
	Wray	EN	EN	-	Ulster	-	-		-	-
	Wren	EN	EN	-	Clare, Cork	-	-		-	-
	Wright	EN	EN	-	Dublin, Mayo, Ulster	-	-		Kincart	IG

* see definitions

Prefix	Surname and Variation	Name Origin*	Migrated From*	Century Estab.	Geographical Locations	Definition of Surname	Language Origin*	Prefix	Pseudonyms and Synonyms	Name Origin*
	Wylie	EN	EN	17th	Clare, Ulster	-	-		-	-
	Wyndham	EN	EN	-	Galway	-	-		-	-
	Wynne	WE	-	-	Dublin, Mayo, Ulster	-	-		-	-
	Wyse	NF	EN	-	Waterford	wiseman	NF		-	-
	Yarr	EN	EN	13th	Antrim, Down	-	-		-	-
	Yeats	EN	EN	17th	Antrim, Dublin, Sligo	dweller by the gate	EN		-	-
	Yorke	EN	EN	17th	Ulster	-	-		-	-
	Young	EN	EN	-	Ulster	-	-		-	-
	Yourell (Eurell)	IG	-	-	Westmeath	-	-		-	-
	Zorkin (Durkin, Durcan)	IG	-	-	Connacht	this is the only Gaelic surname anglicized with a "z"	-		-	-
	Zouche	FR	-	-	Kerry, Limerick	-	-		-	-

* see definitions

IRELAND IN THE 15th CENTURY

IRELAND IN THE LATER FIFTEENTH CENTURY SHOWING BOUNDARIES OF LORDSHIPS.[15]

THE IRISH CLANS OF OLD

The following list of names was given in the Book of Arms, compiled by Sir James Terry, Athlone Herald (1690), now preserved in the British Museum (Harleian MSS. Nos. 4039 & 4040). The names are given exactly as they appear in the list. [16]

Ma	Carty		Mac	Donough
O	Brien		O	Meara
O	Carroll		O	Madden
Ma	Gennis		Mac	Swiny, Baduine
O	Neill		Mac	Gill
O	Donel		O	Maher
Mac	Donel		O	Mulrian
O	Conor, Kerry		Mac	Cartan
O	Seagnasey		Mac	Ailin
Ma	Guire		O	Shanlys
Mac	Murcha		O	Rourke
O	Driscol		O	Suilluan More
O	Dempsy		Mac	Elligot
Mac	Mahon		Mac	Gillycuddy
Ma	Cann		O	Calaghan
O	Dwyer		O	Doude
O	Donel, Ramaltan		Mac	Surdaine
Mac	Gula Padrige		Mac	Brin Na Comora
O	Connor Roe		O	Flaherty
O	Ronan		O	Gara
Mac	Dermot		Mac	Auly
Mac	Swiny Duag		Mac	Quylin
O	Conor Corcmroe		O	Hara
O	Fallan		O	Maloy
Mac	Swiny Fanid		Mac	Auliffe
Mac	Sihy		Mac	Lauglin
Mac	Conor Don		O	Hanlon
O	Dogherty		O	Leary
Mac	Kanna		Mac	Manus

Mac	Gees		Mac	Vadagh
O	Doulee		O	Duin
O	Moriarty		O	Haly
Mac	Egane		Mac	Cabe
Mac	Donough		Mac	Quylin
O	Donoghoue		O	Tuahoil
O	Dougan		O	Brine Carlaugh
Mac	Ennery		Mac	Brine Fin In Linster
Mac	Brouder		Mac	Mile
O	Mahony		O	Daly, Conaught
O	Garuan		O	Brenan
Mac	Coughlan		Mac	Tigernan
Mac	Hugh		Mac	Keou
O	Cullen		O	Kearna, Kilmalok
O	Hogan		O	Haughiern
Mac	Dugoile		Mac	Moylin
Mac	Guillifoyle		Mac	Giolla Finen
O	Callenane		O	Donogane
O	Crowley		O	Foin
Mac	Brien Carigoginel		Mac	Finin Carty
Mac	Gragh		Mac	Brine O Kuonagh
O	Keefe		O	Cullenan
O	Mullane		O	Hart
Mac	Granell		Mac	Keagha
Mac	Rourry		Mac	Caffry
O	Donnauane		O	Floin Arda
O	Finaghty		O	Brine Arra
Mac	Namiee Oflorgon		Mac	Morisch
Mac	Henri		Mac	Kineriny
O	Kearna		O	Connor Failge
O	Draughie siue Dorsy		O	Conor, Sligo
Mac	Cruhin siue Kruhin		Mac	Namara
Mac	Murchoe Coleknock		Mac	Mahon
O	Dulin		O	Dine siue Dunne
O	Gawan		O	Kennedy
Mac	Giarre		Mac	Oda

Mac	Dabhy, Bourk		O	Gorman
O	Kelly		O	Cleirig
O	Cahan		O	Cregan
O	Hagan		O	Reyley
Mac	Shane		O	Malune
Mac	Kallin		O	Brin siue Brrin
O	Mally		O	Bruin
O	Feolane		O	Haullaran
Mac	Colgan		O	Mora
Mac	Groddy		O	Crean
O	Hine		O	Bernes
O	Mulroney siue Mealroney		O	Callins siue O Calane
O	Loclain Bornie		O	Cauanagh
O	Farall			Cinsiolagh Kensillagh
Mac	Adire siue Stapleton		O	Clancy
Mac	Tibbot siue Thibbot Bourk		O	Sehighane
			O	Flanagain
Mac	Seonin Bourk		O	Suilliuan Bear
Mac	Philibin Bourk		O	Cregan
O	Boill		O	Galuan
O	Gormely		O	Crehall
O	Quin		O	Deneen
O	Naughten		O	Laurey
Mac	Vater Bourk		O	Lawlor
Mac	Remon Bourk		O	Hyre
Mac	Richard Bourk		O	Tuohil
Mac	Hubert Bourk		O	Regan
O	Conor		O	Hurly
O	Lonogher		O	Sesnan
O	Hogerta		O	Coglan
O	Crelly		O	Grady
Ma	Condon		O	Cassey
Mac	Padin Bourk		O	Dea
Mac	Euellin		O	Loinsig
Mac	Maoilre Bourk		O	Beallan
Mac	Vghak Bourk		O	Nelan

O	Deorane		O	Sunigan
O	Moylan		O	Donnolan
O	Linin		O	Feiniela
O	Conaly		O	Fogerty
O	Halpin		O	Bruodin
O	Scanlan		O	Conry
O	Mullony		O	Considin
O	Lounders		O	Enos
O	Boughelly		O	Brady
O	Cormcane		O	Heher
O	Kenelly		O	Hernan
O	Higgin		O	Hegerty
O	Mehegan		O	Cormacan
Mac	Geohegaine		O	Gripha
Mac	Guillegan		O	Sinan
Mac	Cauhil Irights		O	Krihone
Mac	Quard item		O	Henraughty
Mac	Nielus item		O	Connell
Mac	Donnells Galoglagh		O	Schanla
Mac	Closkey item		O	Huologhan
Mac	Gork Termanagh		O	Hainin
Mac	Gabfraigh item		O	Horain
Mac	Gennis Kiluuarlin		O	Conceanain
Mac	Deuett		O	Moran
Mac	Ward		O	Malry
Mac	Erige		O	Mogair
Mac	Machon		O	Sinnagh siue Fox
Mac	Flanncha		O	Morrij
O	Melaghlen siue Mlachlein		O	Cullinan
			O	Coruin
O	Malaghlin		O	Uilcuth
O	Dougan		O	Multulle
O	Nuolan		O	Culin
O	Duigenan		O	Caishin
O	Delany		O	Flinn
O	Galchor		O	Suridin siue Sheridan

O	Castuly	O	Considin
O	Forehane	O	Shea
O	Cussin	O	Freel Termanagh
O	Coultan	O	Nahan, supr T
O	Meoilbraenoin	O	Diry, supr T
O	Toma	O	Duffy
O	Faluey	O	Mallan T
O	Shiels	O	Mungan T
O	Hefernan	O	Duuin T
O	Ferenan	O	Onnelly T
O	Hederiman	O	Gilriagh
O	Houragne		Duigenan
O	Goran	O	Tyernan
O	Cullinan	O	Cowhy
O	Boughaula	O	Duilcuth
O	Spilan		Nogolough
O	Brisane		Beatheach
O	Rerdane	Mac	Brine Fin In Linster
O	Hannan	Mac	Iames
O	Line		

THE MOST POPULAR SURNAMES IN IRELAND

The following list reflects the one hundred most popular surnames in Ireland as of 1890. The names are listed numerically, according to the estimated popluation bearing each surname. In addition, the ethnic origin of each surname is also reflected. [17]

Rank in Population	Surname	Est. Population Bearing each name	Ethnic Origin
1.	Murphy	62,600	Irish
2.	Kelly	55,900	Irish
3.	Sullivan	43,600	Irish
4.	Walsh	41,700	Irish
5.	Smith	33,700	English
6.	O'Brien	33,400	Irish
7.	Byrne	33,300	Irish
8.	Ryan	32,000	Irish
9.	Connor	31,200	Irish
10.	O'Neill	29,100	Irish
11.	Reilly	29,000	Irish
12.	Doyle	23,000	Norse
13.	MacCarthy	22,300	Irish
14.	Gallagher	21,800	Irish
15.	Doherty	20,800	Irish
16.	Kennedy	19,900	Irish

Rank in Population	Surname	Est. Population Bearing each name	Ethnic Origin
17.	Lynch	19,800	Irish/Norman
18.	Murray	19,600	Irish/Scottish
19.	Quinn	18,200	Irish
20.	Moore	17,700	English
21.	MacLaughlin	17,500	Irish
22.	Carroll	17,400	Irish
23.	Connolly	17,000	Irish
24.	Daly	17,000	Irish
25.	Connell	16,600	Irish
26.	Wilson	16,300	English
27.	Dunne	16,300	Irish
28.	Brennan	16,000	Irish
29.	Burke	15,900	Norman
30.	Collins	15,700	English
31.	Campbell	15,600	Irish/Scottish
32.	Clarke	15,400	English
33.	Johnston	15,200	English
34.	Hughes	14,900	Irish
35.	Farrell	14,700	Irish
36.	Fitzgerald	14,700	Norman
37.	Brown	14,600	Norman
38.	Martin	14,600	English/Irish

Rank in Population	Surname	Est. Population Bearing each name	Ethnic Origin
39.	Maguire	14,400	Irish
40.	Nolan	14,300	Irish
41.	Flynn	14,300	Irish
42.	Thompson	14,200	English
43.	Callaghan	14,200	Irish
44.	O' Donnell	13,900	Irish
45.	Duffy	13,600	Irish
46.	Mahony	13,500	Irish
47.	Boyle	13,000	Irish
48.	Healy	13,000	Irish
49.	Shea	13,000	Irish
50.	White	13,000	English
51.	Sweeney	12,500	Irish
52.	Hayes	12,300	Norman
53.	Kavanagh	12,200	Irish
54.	Power	12,100	Norman
55.	Mac Grath	11,900	Irish
56.	Moran	11,800	Irish
57.	Brady	11,600	Irish
58.	Stewart	11,400	Scottish
59.	Casey	11,300	Irish
60.	Foley	11,200	Irish

Rank in Population	Surname	Est. Population Bearing each name	Ethnic Origin
61.	Fitzpatrick	11,100	Irish
62.	Leary	11,000	Irish
63.	Mc Donnell	11,000	Irish
64.	Mc Mahon	10,700	Irish
65.	Donnelly	10,700	Irish
66.	Regan	10,500	Irish
67.	Donovan	9,900	Irish
68.	Burns	9,800	Scottish
69.	Flanagan	9,800	Irish
70.	Mullan	9,800	Irish
71.	Barry	9,700	Norman
72.	Kane	9,700	Irish
73.	Robinson	9,700	English
74.	Cunningham	9,600	Scottish
75.	Griffin	9,600	Irish
76.	Kenny	9,600	Irish
77.	Sheehan	9,600	Irish
78.	Ward	9,500	Irish
79.	Whelan	9,500	Irish
80.	Lyons	9,400	English
81.	Reid	9,200	English
82.	Graham	9,100	Scottish

Rank in Population	Surname	Est. Population Bearing each name	Ethnic Origin
83.	Higgins	9,100	Irish
84.	Cullen	9,000	Irish
85.	Keane	9,000	Irish
86.	King	9,000	English
87.	Maher	9,000	Irish
88.	Mac Kenna	9,000	Irish
89.	Bell	8,800	French
90.	Scott	8,700	English
91.	Hogan	8,600	Irish
92.	Keefe	8,600	Irish
93.	Magee	8,600	Irish
94.	Mac Namara	8,600	Irish
95.	Mac Donald	8,500	Scottish
96.	Mac Dermott	8,400	Irish
97.	Maloney	8,300	Irish
98.	Rourke	8,300	Irish
99.	Buckley	8,200	English
100.	Dwyer	8,100	Irish

THE IRISH CHIEFTAINS
NOW AND THEN

It has been said many times over that every true Irishman is a descendant of an Irish king. Some people may accept this as fact; then there are those who would consider this a moot matter. Regardless whether it's true or not, the following information has a tendency to lend a ton of credence in favor of this claim. And, when one seriously considers the clan structure, with its sub-clans, sub-sub-clans and other tentacles of extended family structure, we could all very well be descendants of Irish chieftains --- at least.

The last official statement of authentic chiefs was made in 1956. It has been brought up-to-date in a work entitled "The Irish Chiefs" by C. Eugene Swezey (New York 1974) where information regarding present addresses, heirs, arms, etc. will be found. In that work the prefix "The" before the surname is given because it has been used in English to designate them (as it was in Irish in the case of hibernicized Norman septs or clans). In their signatures however, the surname alone is used without Christian names. [18]

NOW . . .

Those now officially recognized are:

O'Brien of Thomond	Fox (An Sionnach)
O'Callaghan	MacGillycuddy of the Reeks
O'Connor Don	O'Grady of Kilballyowen
MacDermot of Coolavain	O'Kelly of Gallagh
MacDermot Roe	O'Morchoe
O'Donnell of Tirconnell	MacMorrough Kavanagh
O'Donoghue of the Glens	O'Neill of Clanaboy
O'Donovan	O'Toole of Fir Tire

Before the final submergence of the Brehon system of government in Ireland there were, needless to say, many more recognized chiefs than the sixteen listed above who have acutally substantiated their claim in recent times. Sixteenth century sources, such as State Papers and the Fiants (warrants to the Chancery Authority for the issue of letters patent under the Great Seal. They dealt with matters ranging from commissions for appointments to high office and important government activities to grants of *English liberty and pardons to the humblest of the native Irish*).[19]* These documents show the heads of the following families where there refered to as chiefs:

...AND THEN

MacArtan (Now MacCarton)
MacAuliffe
MacAuley
O' Beirne
O' Boyle (Not akin to the English Boyle, Earl of Cork)
O' Brennan
O' Byrne
O' Cahan (Kane)
O' Carroll
MacCarthy Reagh
MacClancy
O' Clery
MacCoughlan
O' Connell
O' Connolly
O' Conor Faly
O' Conor Roe
O' Conor Sligo
O' Daly
O' Dempsey
O' Devlin
O' Doherty
O' Loughlin

MacDonagh
O' Dowd
O' Driscoll
O' Dunn
O' Dwyer
O' Farrell
O' Flaherty
O' Folane
O' Gara
MacGeoghagen
MacGorman
MacGrath
MacGuiness
O' Hagan
O' Hanlon
O' Hara
O' Heyne
O' Keefe
MacKenna
O' Kennedy
MacKiernan
MacKinnane (Ford)
MacLoughlin
O' Mulvey

* Comments in parenthesis this author's.

O' Madden
MacMahon
O' Mahony
O' Malley
O' Malloy
O' Mannin
MacManus
O' Melaghlin
O' More
O' Mulryan (Ryan)

MacNamara
O' Nolan
O' Phelin
O' Reilly
MacRory
O' Rourke
O' Shaughnessy
O' Sheridan
O' Sullivan Beare
O' Sullivan Mor

NOTES

(1) Mitchell, Brian A., A New Genealogical Atlas of Ireland, (Baltimore, Maryland: Genealogical Publishing Company, 1986) Third printing 1992, p. 13.

(2) Ryan, James D. Irish Records Sources for Family and Local History, (Salt Lake City, Utah: Ancestry Inc., 1988), p. x/vii.

(3) Foster, R.F., The Oxford Illustrated History of Ireland, (New York, NY: Oxford University Press, 1991), p. 38. (By permission of Oxford Univeristy Press.)

(4) Ryan, Irish Records Sources for Family and Local History, p. x/vii.

(5) Foster, The Oxford Illustrated History of Ireland, p. 53. (By permission of Oxford Univeristy Press.)

(6) Foster, The Oxford Illustrated History of Ireland, pp. 56-57. (By permission of Oxford Univeristy Press.)

(7) Ryan, Irish Records Sources for Family and Local History, p. x/vii.

(8) Ryan, Irish Records Sources for Family and Local History, p. v/ii.

(9) Ryan, Irish Records Sources for Family and Local History, pp. x/vii - x/viii.

(10) Matheson, Robert E., Surnames of Ireland (Together With) Surnames and Christian Names in Ireland, (Reprinted by Genealogical Publishing Company, Baltimore, Maryland, 1988), pp. 30-31. (1909).

(11) MacLysaght, Edward, Irish Families, (Blackrock, County Dublin, Republic of Ireland: Irish Academic Press Ltd., 1991) pp. 15-16.

(12) Matheson, Surnames of Ireland (Together With) Surnames and Christian Names in Ireland, pp. 17-18, (1901).

(13) MacLysaght, Irish Families, pp. 21-24.

(14) MacLysaght, Irish Families, p. 23.

(15) Foster, Oxford Illustrated History of Ireland, p. 93. (By permission of Oxford Univeristy Press.)

(16) Matheson, Surnames of Ireland (Together with) Surnames and Christian Names in Ireland, pp. 76-78 (1909).

(17) Matheson, Surnames of Ireland (Together with) Surnames and Christian Names of Ireland, pp. 7-8 (1909).

(18) MacLysaght, Edward, More Irish Families (Irish Academic Press Ltd., Blackrock, County Dublin, Republic of Ireland, 1985), p. 20.

(19) MacLysaght, Edward, The Surnames of Ireland (Irish Academic Press Ltd., Blackrock, County Dublin, Republic of Ireland, Sixth Edition, 1985), p. xix.

A RECOMMENDED READING LIST

The Pulications listed below contain their own bibliographies, all of which would be of great assistance to those readers who wish to pursue this subject matter.

Delaney, Mary Murray, Our Irish Ways, (Dillon Press Inc., 500 South Third St., Minneapolis, Minnesota 55415, 1973) (Paperback)

Durning, William and Mary, A Guide to Irish Roots, (Irish Family Name Society, La Mesa, California, 1986).

Mac Lysaght, Edward, The Surnames of Ireland, Sixth Edition, (Irish Academic Press, Ltd., Blackrock, County Dublin, Ireland, 1985)

Mac Lysaght, Edward, Irish Families, Fourth Edition, (Irish Academic Press, Ltd., Blackrock, County Dublin, Ireland, 1991)

Mac Lysaght, Edward, More Irish Families, (Irish Academic Press Ltd., Blackrock, County Dublin, Ireland, 1982)

Matheson, Robert E., Special Report on Surnames In Ireland (1909) (Together with) Varieties and Synonyms of Surnames and Christian Names Ireland (1901). Reprinted by Genealogical Publishing Co., Baltimore, MD, 1992)

Mitchell, Bryan, A New Genealogical Atlas of Ireland, (Genealogical Publishing Co., Baltimore, MD, 1986)

O' Laughlin, Michael C., The Book of Irish Families Great and Small, (Irish Geneological Foundation, Kansas City, MO, 1992)

O' Laughlin, Michael C., Master Book of Irish Surnames, (Irish Geneological Foundation, Kansas City, MO, 1993)

Ryan, James D., Irish Records Sources for Family and Local History (Ancestry Inc., Salt Lake City, Utah, 1988)

Wibberly, Leonard Patrick O' Connor, The Coming of the Green, (Henry Holt and Company, New York, NY, 1958)

Woulfe, Patrick Rev., Irish Names and Surnames, (Kilmallock, Ireland, 1923, Special Revised Edition, Irish Geneological Foundation, Kansas City, MO, 1992)

In addition to the preceding reading list, the following addresses will also prove invaluable sources of information:

    Directories of Roman Catholic Registers in Ireland by David McElroy.

    Directories of Presbyterian Church Registers by David McElroy.

    The National Archives, Four Courts, Arran Quay, Dublin 7, Ireland.

    General Register Office, Joyce House, 8/11 Lombard Street East, Dublin 2, Ireland.

    State Paper Office, Dublin Castle, Dublin 2, Ireland.

    Genealogical Office, Kildare Street, Dublin 2, Ireland.

    National Library of Ireland, Kildare Street, Dublin 2, Ireland.

    Registry of Deeds, Henrietta Street, Dublin 7, Ireland.

As of 1989 Genealogy Centers have been established in all the counties of Ireland except Cavan, Dublin, Laois, Louth, Monaghan, and Westmeath. All counties expect to have such centers by 1994. At present I do not have the addresses for these centers but if you will write Bord Failte, Baggot Street Bridge, Dublin 2, Ireland or phone (01) 765871 they will provide this information to you.

A new office, Clans of Ireland, has opened at 2 Kildare Street, Dublin 2, Ireland, Phone (01) 618811. Eighty-seven clans had registered with the office as of 1 March 1991 and twenty-eight clan rallies were held in various parts of Ireland in 1991. If contacted, the Clans of Ireland office will provide you, at no cost, the dates and locations of planned rallies. Obviously, a Clan Rally should provide a mother lode of information on your family antecedents as well as living relatives.

If your ancestors came from the province of Ulster (see map on page x), the following addresses will be helpful:

    Public Record Office of Northern Ireland, 66 Balmoral Avenue, Belfast BT1, Northern Ireland.

    General Register Office, Oxford House, Chichester Street, Belfast BT1, Northern Ireland.

    Linenhall Library, Donegall Square, Belfast BT1, Northern Ireland.

Publications that will help in your American research that may be ordered from the Consumer Information Center-2B, P.O. Box 100, Pueblo, Colorado 81002 are:

    Where to Write for Vital Records. (This gives you the addresses to write in each state where you can obtain Birth, Death, Marriage, Divorce records and the cost of each.)

    Directory of U.S. Government Depository Libraries.

    Your Right to Federal Records.

    Using Records in the National Archives for Genealogical Research.

Contrary to the name we go by, or where we call home, being Irish, like a credo, dwells only in the mind and heart of the believer! jo...

www.ingramcontent.com/pod-product-compliance
Lightning Source LLC
Chambersburg PA
CBHW080736300426
44114CB00019B/2612

50% OFF!

HESI® A² ONLINE TEST PREP COURSE

We consider it an honor and a privilege that you chose our HESI® A² Study Guide. As a way of showing our appreciation and to help us better serve you, we have partnered with Mometrix Test Preparation to offer you 50% off their online HESI® A² Prep Course.

Mometrix has structured their online course to perfectly complement your printed study guide. Many HESI® A² courses are needlessly expensive and don't deliver enough value. With their course, you get access to the best HESI® A² prep material, and you only pay half price.

WHAT'S IN THE HESI® A² TEST PREP COURSE?

- ✓ **HESI® A² Study Guide**: Get access to content that complements your study guide.

- ✓ **Progress Tracker**: Their customized course allows you to check off content you have studied or feel confident with.

- ✓ **3,350+ Practice Questions**: With 3,350+ practice questions and lesson reviews, you can test yourself again and again to build confidence.

- ✓ **HESI® A² Flashcards**: Their course includes a flashcard mode consisting of over 550 content cards to help you study.

TO RECEIVE THIS DISCOUNT, VISIT THE WEBSITE AT

link.mometrix.com/hesi

USE THE DISCOUNT CODE:
STARTSTUDYING

IF YOU HAVE ANY QUESTIONS OR CONCERNS, PLEASE CONTACT MOMETRIX AT SUPPORT@MOMETRIX.COM

Mometrix ONLINE COURSES